Stackpole arms and armour illustrated monographs

Percussion Guns & Rifles

1. 'The Old Shekarry', H. A. Leveson, in his ideal sporting costume of 1867.

D. W. BAILEY

Percussion Guns & Rifles

an illustrated reference guide

Portland Public Library

STACKPOLE BOOKS

First published in the U.S.A. in 1972 by
Stackpole Books,
Cameron and Kelker Streets,
Harrisburg,
Pennsylvania 17105

Printed in Great Britain

Library of Congress Cataloging in Publication Data

Bailey, De Witt.
    Percussion guns & rifles.

    (Stackpole arms and armour illustrated monographs)
    Bibliography: p.
    1. Firearms. 2. Firearms--Locks. I. Title.
TS536.6.M8B35   683'.42'09034   72-6794
ISBN 0-8117-1242-7

Contents

Acknowledgements

The kind co-operation of the entire staff of H. M. Tower of London Armouries has made this work possible. I should particularly like to express my gratitude to A. R. Dufty, Esq., A.R.I.B.A., F.S.A., Master of the Armouries, for permitting me to research amongst the specimens held in the Tower collections. I am also very grateful to A. N. Kennard, Esq., B.A., F.S.A., and to Howard Blackmore, Esq., for the benefit of their knowledge.

I am indebted to Messrs. Jeremy Hall and S. F. Scorey, and to Studio M of Teddington, for the fine photography which graces this book. All of the photographs are Crown Copyright and appear by the kind permission of the Department of the Environment, except those which appear by permission of the Smithsonian Institution, Washington D.C. (plates 24, 43, 67 and 68), that which appears by permission of the Historisches Museum, Frauenfeld, Switzerland (plate 42) and plates taken from weapons in private hands (plates 11, 27–32, 34, 44–52, and 75).

I would also like to express my gratitude to those who gave of their time to provide access to weapons in their collections or to provide illustrations, amongst them Messrs. E. J. Burton, Geoffrey Boothroyd, Eugen Heer, E. J. Holmes, C. J. Paring, M. O. A. Stanton and D. B. Tubbs.

Despite the help and assistance I have received from many sources, I must—of course—add that the responsibility for any faults that may ultimately be found is mine alone.

Introduction

As a mechanism in general use for the ignition of all forms of firearms, the flintlock held a virtual monopoly for more than two hundred years. Once established (at the beginning of the seventeenth century) no serious efforts were made to replace the flint and steel principle except for a very small number of individual experiments attempted during the late eighteenth century. No one involved in the everyday use of firearms considered that any improvement was possible in the basic system; from the technical viewpoint the guns had been brought to the highest possible state of development by the beginning of the nineteenth century. A very strong feeling of complacence and satisfaction prevailed amongst the users of firearms with regard to the ignition system, and it is therefore far from surprising that the revolutionary developments of Alexander Forsyth were greeted with no particular acclaim and were not readily accepted. It is no exaggeration to state that, while Forsyth's percussion system went into commercial production in 1808, the flintlock remained in widespread use throughout the world for the greater part of the period 1810–50; in the less civilised tracts of the world, the percussion lock had scarcely been introduced by 1850 in hands other than those of particular individuals.

The sporting gun and the pistol were the first two categories of smallarms to which the percussion ignition system was widely applied and in which it was early accepted. The certainty and rapidity of ignition—when compared to the flintlock—made it highly desirable in a weapon used on flying targets: it lessened the number of miss-fires and consequently of lost birds, and the problem of lead became less acute with the faster lock time. The simplicity and compactness of the new system recommended it for use on pistols.

Had the original Forsyth system remained to promote the obvious advantages of the percussion system, it might never have gone further; until less complicated and delicate means were found to apply it, the percussion system possessed few practical advantages over the flintlock although—provided that the mechanism was kept in perfect order and that undue wear did not mar the operation—Forsyth's system possessed rapidity of ignition and greater resistance to weather conditions. It was not until more efficient and less complex means of applying the principle were developed that it was widely advocated by persons other than those who could afford the theoretical excellence of the idea without being unduly inconvenienced by its drawbacks. With this in mind, the years 1816 and 1818, as well as 1821, should be considered as important in the history of the percussion system as 1805, the year in which Forsyth first announced

7

his discoveries. In 1816 Joshua Shaw's copper cap made its commercial appearance in the shop of Joseph Egg, and it was on 3rd August 1818 that Joseph Manton patented his tube-lock—the other form of percussion ignition which survived the early years. No real progress was made in the commercial distribution of the percussion principle because Forsyth and Company, resorting to litigation, successfully blocked all possible infringements of their 1807 patent. For this reason 1821, the year in which the patent expired, is of particular importance. Almost immediately, on 10th November, William Westley Richards received a patent for a magazine primer. The first mention in a British patent of a copper cap appeared in John Day's patent of November 1823, granted to protect the mechanism of a walking-stick gun. Another major step forward was made in the perfection of the percussion principle in the same year, when E. Goode Wright of Hereford disclosed in a letter to *The Philosophical Magazine* how he had applied mercury fulminate to copper percussion caps, thereby eliminating the far more corrosive potassium chlorate previously employed. By 1824 all of the fundamental developments in the percussion system had taken place.

Sporting Guns

The appearance of the modern 'English' sporting gun had been established during the later years of the Regency period, and it has not changed significantly to the present day. Certain modifications were made to the form of the stock when back-action locks were employed, but these affect the appearance little more than some early breech-loading systems.

The double-barrelled percussion gun is most often seen today, simply because the single-barrelled sporting guns were generally made in much cheaper quality, much larger numbers, and were much more heavily worked: they did not survive, and as they were expended so they were laid aside. Although there were far more single guns made than double guns, fine quality single-barrelled guns are considerably scarcer than doubles of equivalent quality. Single guns had but a limited appeal to the gentleman sportsman during the percussion period, and were generally limited to short-barrelled covert guns, long-barrelled live pigeon guns, and to extremely large and heavy wildfowling guns. The single gun played a very important rôle in the export market to North America, South Africa and Australia, into which continents they were sold for a few shillings. The earlier single-barrelled percussion guns were similar in construction and decoration to their flintlock predecessors; the scroll trigger-guard continued to be popular well into the 1840s on the single gun, even though it fell from general use on the double gun. The cheekrest fell into disuse, and ramrods became stouter as wadding became heavier and thicker. Barrel keys (wedges or slides) were surrounded with silver or German silver escutcheons which in the early years, until c. 1830, were octagonal or square then tended to an oval form. The wrist was often chequered with a flat design used on flint guns, but the fore-end was normally left plain. The average percussion single-barrelled gun was of 12 bore, or slightly larger than the average 14 bore of the double gun. Their advantages were considered to be speed of handling in covert for pheasants and their ability to stand heavy charges for the occasional long shot. The single gun intended for the home market averaged a 32in barrel, and covert guns had barrels as short as 26in—not a generally recommended type.

The back-action lock appeared early in the 1820s on guns by the top London makers but, despite several superficial advantages, it was not 'stylish' and could not maintain itself against the more pleasing lines of the bar-lock and the side-lock. It was also held by some sportsmen to be weaker and slower in its action than the conventional patterns. It retained a place in the cheap gun market because thinner stock blanks could be used with it and there was less stock carving and finishing. Back-action locks continued to be used on best guns made throughout the percussion period —at the customer's whim.

The first decade of the serious commercial production in England of the percussion gun saw the introduction and failure of a number of systems based upon pills or pellets, patches, magazines of the improved Forsyth pattern, and several types of tubes. Although some, amongst them Charles Moore's pill-lock, seem to have enjoyed a few seasons' vogue, only a small number stood the test of time. The most important of these (aside from the common copper cap which emerged as the standard) were Manton's 1818 pattern tube-lock, Samuel and Charles Smith's 1830-patented 'Imperial cap', and Westley Richards' steel-tube lock which appeared in 1831. Manton's tube-lock, together with Joseph Egg's copper cap, had been granted a Government trial as early as 1820.

The average English double gun was made with 30in barrels and in 14 bore, although both 12 and 16 bores were also popular. The trend was decidedly away from the 18 and 20 bores of the flintlock period and towards shorter barrels, but the foregoing figures stand as the period's average.

'English' sporting guns, unless specifically so ordered for use with patched ball, were not cylinder bored. A variety of tapers and counterbores were employed by the various barrel makers and the gun makers themselves, the details of which constituted trade secrets jealously guarded by all to whom they were known. A firm's reputation would depend upon how well their guns shot; much time and effort was spent in the final polishing of barrels to ensure certain constant and flawless tapers, and to make them group well. Cheaper guns did not have this degree of internal finish, but it is a mistake to consider that all guns made before the invention of 'true choke boring' were plain cylinder bores.

Virtually all American double-barrelled percussion guns were manufactured either in England or in Belgium; those few which were assembled in America used English or Belgian barrels and English locks. A greater proportion of the single-barrelled guns were made or assembled in America, but once again the majority came from European sources which manufactured them to the standards required for rough usage. Individual examples of indigenous sporting guns will be found in America, but the economic realities of the time dictated that importation was the only practical means of supplying the demand for sporting guns prior to the era of the machine-made breech-loading gun. Guns for the American market tended to be of 12 bore and larger, with barrels of 30in and longer. There was little decoration on the majority of these guns aside from border lines engraved upon the lockplates and furniture, but the occasional scroll engraving was at best of mediocre quality. The guns were heavily and soundly built, made for hard service rather than elegant handling under ideal conditions; the barrels were often held by two keys rather than one. One of two favourite devices used for the American market was to mark the name of a famous maker, such as MANTON, MOORE, RICHARDS or SCOTT and LONDON—omitting the address—and the other was to engrave upon the rib LONDON FINE TWIST or FINE DAMASCUS or a similar variation

10

on the theme. These ruses were employed by both English and Belgian manufacturers.

The outstanding characteristic of the Continental percussion sporting gun, whether single or double-barrelled, was the lavish and ornate decoration which graced the stock and often the locks. To non-Continental eyes much of this appeared garish and grotesque, but much of it was extremely well executed. Neo-Gothic patterns predominated, intertwined with animals' heads and mythical figures, foliage and vinework. French and Belgian guns often had a long rounded semi-pistol grip, with the base finished as a mythical head. German guns frequently had a scroll guard with the entire bow and grip formed of horn, while in others a semi-pistolgrip was finished as an animal head. Single-barrelled guns had half-length stocks without ribs beneath the barrels, in these the rod pipes were merely soldered to the underside of the barrel. Double guns sometimes had half-octagonal or 'Spanish-form' barrels rather than the conventional round barrels. Eyes for sling swivels were almost invariably present on all Continental sporting guns. Back-action locks were as much in use on the cheaper guns as in Britain and it is also true that a limited number of first quality guns were made with back-action locks—a larger proportion than in Britain. Gold inlay work was very popular, even on guns with little other ornamentation.

In their development from the flintlock, Continental sporting guns followed roughly similar lines to the English arms; copies of the Forsyth system appeared in France c. 1810 and by the 1820s the copper cap was the primary form of percussion ignition in use on the Continent, although still in a world in which the flintlock held dominance. Bore sizes tended to remain smaller, 16 bore being about the largest, 20 bore closer to the average, and barrel lengths were longer at an average of 32in—both being continuations of flintlock styles. The percussion system suffered an early demise on the Continent, especially on sporting guns, owing to the successful introduction in France of the pin-fire cartridge and the Lefaucheaux breech-loading mechanism.

2

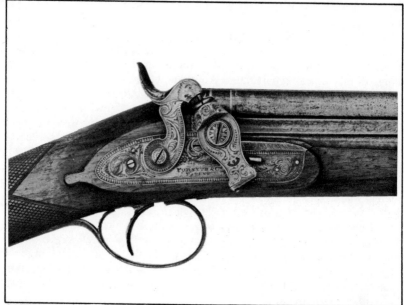

2. The Forsyth 'roller primer' lock, 1808. The loose fulminating powder was contained in the bottle-like magazine fitting on to a spindle, which was also the pan. The bottle was turned over by hand to deposit a charge of powder in the pan cavity of the spindle. The roller and piston had to be kept carefully cleaned and lubricated, and the piston springs had to be periodically replaced. Special tools were required for dismantling and cleaning the lock, which in use was far more complicated—if somewhat more reliable and weatherproof —than the flintlock.

3. Joseph Manton's tube-lock, 1818. This was the first successfully-marketed competition for the Forsyth lock and the system continued to be popular for most of the percussion period in competition with the copper cap. It was particularly favoured by live-pigeon shooters and wild-fowlers, where absolute reliability was essential. The tube is held against the vent by the tube-holder, and is struck through a cavity by the nose of the hammer.

4. William Westley Richards' patent magazine-primer lock, 1821. The first

mechanism patented after the expiration of Forsyth's patent, it represents little improvement except that priming is automatically accomplished, and that the magazine is thrown back and closed on the fall of the hammer.

5. Charles Moore's pill-lock was amongst the most popular of this type of percussion ignition; the pills were placed in the cavity of the pan either by hand or from a specially designed dispenser. The lock could also utilise copper caps by changing the removable striker in the hammer nose and screwing a nipple in place of the pan-like nipple of the pill mechanism.

6. Another early copper cap gun. The awkward form of the hammer with a small nose and wide flat body is typical of cap guns made during the 1820s by many leading London makers. Three holes pierce the platinum plug of the breech, which were supposed to lessen the force of the recoil, to prevent excessive pressure at the moment of explosion, to reduce fouling by admitting oxygen into the breech to facilitate complete combustion, and to make loading easier by preventing trapped air keeping the wadding from the powder and shot.

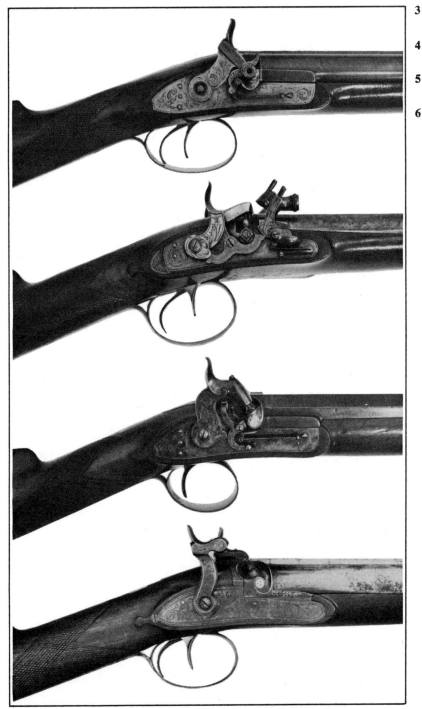

Sporting Guns

7. The back-action lock was considered a great improvement over the bar-lock at the time of its first appearance in the early 1820s. It was held to strengthen the wrist of the gun, to render the working parts completely waterproof, and to prevent fouling and corrosive gases from the breech penetrating the lockwork.

8. An unmarked German pill-lock/ cap-lock, with a reversible striker nose inside the magazine-head of the hammer. The holder at the front of the lock is withdrawn by the grip lever just prior to firing. The nipple may utilise both pill and cap, as the pill is held in the hammer nose and carried to the nipple for detonation.

9. An Austrian pill-lock by Mayer of Vienna. The mechanism (developed by Prosser of London as an improvement over Forsyth's system) operates automatically with the cocking of the hammer, when the magazine pivots forward and drops a pill into the pan cavity. The fall of the hammer revolves the magazine into the position shown. The trigger guard of this example is missing.

10. Samuel and Charles Smith's 'Imperial Nipple and Cap', patented 1830. The object was to reduce the length of travel of the cap flame, thereby reducing the area open to corrosion, and to make the cap larger and easier to handle. It remained popular for the duration of the percussion period on both sporting guns and rifles. The hammer nose and nipple were removable with special tools, and could be easily replaced with a conventional nose and nipple.

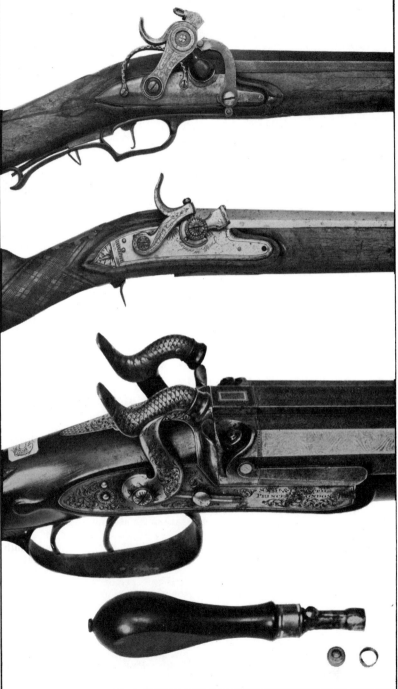

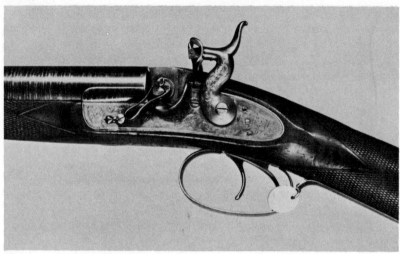

11

11. A spring-clip tube-lock mechanism popular from the early 1830s, which vied with Manton's 1818 device as the 'most popular tube-lock', until both were replaced in public regard after 1840 by Westley Richards' steel tube primer-lock.

12. This double-barrelled 14 bore Purdey, of 1824, shows the lines of the classic 'English' double gun fully developed by the beginning of the percussion period. The large-bow guard and scroll grip are survivals from the flintlock era which continued as late as the mid-1840s.

13. The single-barrelled gun declined greatly in popularity amongst the British sporting gentry, relegated to the status of a specialised arm for covert shooting or—in large sizes— wild-fowling and live-pigeon shooting. As an export arm, however, they continued to be made in very large numbers. This fine quality 14 bore by Clough and Sons of Bath, *c.* 1828, is fitted with Somerville's Patent Safety. The lock and trigger are locked until the flat front of the guard, which has a lever pivoted at its bottom edge, is

pressed back by the shooter's hand; placing the hand against the front of the guard rather than along the fore-end was highly recommended in the early percussion era, when the bursting of barrels at the breech was common. It was also held to give better control of the gun.

14. The classic 'Blue Rock' gun, used for live-pigeon shooting matches. The 10 bore barrel with heavy breech, nipper-spring tube-lock, spur-guard, and lack of ramrod (a stout loading rod was separately carried) are characteristic of this style of weapon. This splendid example by William Reavell of the Strand, *c.* 1844, has fully engraved steel furniture and a heavy cast silver fore-end cap.

15. The percussion shotgun in America was normally of English or Belgian manufacture; what local production there was being generally assembled from imported barrels, locks and (sometimes) furniture. This Belgian 10 bore is typical of the best quality exported to America and is engraved on the rib—in the English style—PHILADELPHIA.

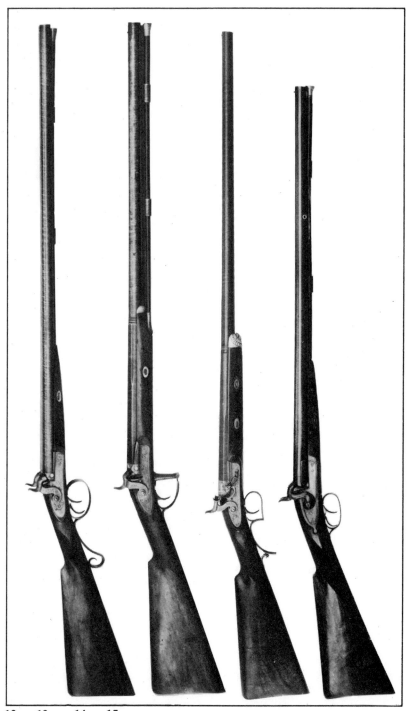

12, 13, 14, 15

17

Sporting Guns

16. A Belgian double 10 bore for the American market with 36in barrels and back-action locks. This pattern was also exported to the Indian market where the same rough conditions and longer ranges applied. Many guns which at first glance appear 'English' are in fact Belgian-made in the English style as often for sale in Britain as for export to the colonies.

17. A Continental percussion sporting gun. This weapon shows the typical features of its type—long barrels of small bore, back-action locks with faceted hammers and stocks with a considerable drop in the butt. The basic ideas were executed on arms of widely-differing quality, with various neo-Gothic engraving added to suit the whim of the customer or the demands of the market. Guns without external marks were usually export weapons; those intended for the domestic market, generally named, were usually of superior finish and more tastefully decorated. The German and Austrian guns often have trigger guards carved of wood or horn, and scroll grips. The ordinary Continental guns are not nearly so grotesque as so often implied: much of the First Empire style had faded by the mid-percussion era, and was retained only for de luxe arms and for the export trade at the other extreme.

18. A 14 bore by Meyer of Brussels, c. 1840. The 'English' influence gained some hold on Continental design during the percussion period, evident in the clean and simple lines of this high-quality double. The breeches are inlaid with silver, and the maker's name and address are inlaid in gold on the locks. The inscription DAMAS DE PARIS is inlaid in gold on the barrel rib. The steel furniture is very much in the 'English' style although engraved in the Continental fashion.

19. A large-bore 'cripple stopper' by Pether of Oxford. When a punt-gun had brought down large numbers of birds with a single shot, many remained alive though unable to fly. This 'cripple stopper' was employed to finish the wounded birds at close range. The bore measures 1 9/16in, and the barrel is 32in long. Guns of this style and size, but with much longer barrels, were used as shoulder punt-guns by British and American wildfowlers throughout the nineteenth century. This example is a drum conversion from flintlock.

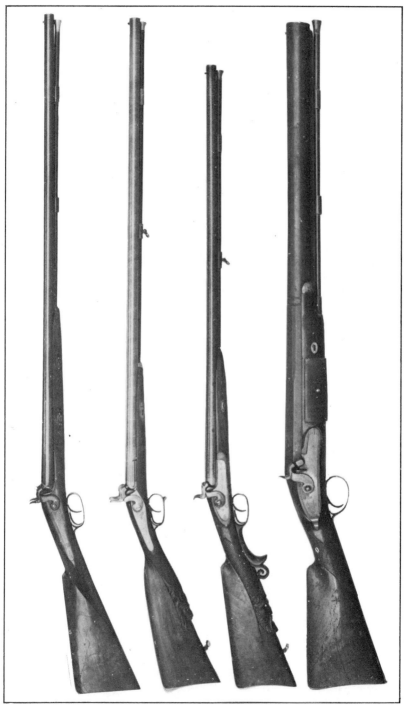

16,   17,   18,   19

Sporting Rifles

There can be no doubt that both numerically and stylistically the Americans produced the greatest number of percussion sporting rifles. The great age of the Pennsylvania longrifle had passed by the time the percussion system gained a strong following in the United States in the 1830s, but there were still a considerable number of archaic full-stocked and heavily decorated rifles of this type being made. Recent scholarship has divided the many forms of American sporting rifles into distinct regional types including the New England rifle, the New York State rifle, the Ohio Valley rifle, the Pennsylvania longrifle, the Mountain rifle, and the Plains rifle—to mention only the most important. By the 1840s all of these types except the last featured a small bore ranging in diameter from 0.25in to 0.45in, and all were used primarily for small game shooting. The regional variations were usually expressed in the shape and material of the stocks, and in the material, style and decoration of the furniture.

The New England rifle was most usually half-stocked, and often with a chequered wrist; a back-action lock was sometimes fitted, and brass furniture occasionally replaced the more popular German silver furniture and inlays which decorated the stock. Scroll engraving commonly appeared on the furniture. The rifles of New York State were stocked in cherrywood, with brass furniture; rifles of the Ohio Valley had half-length stocks of curly maple with furniture of brass. The Mountain rifle was characterised by a minimum of furniture, and often lacked butt and toeplates; a simple hole drilled into the butt's side contained grease, and replaced the elaborate patchboxes found on other regional varieties. The furniture of the Mountain rifles was generally of crudely cast or wrought iron, and the stocks were of maple, ash or walnut—of half or full-length.

The most popular and best-known of American percussion sporting rifles was the Plains rifle, exemplified by the Hawken rifle as made in Saint Louis, Missouri, in the period 1825–65. They were heavy rifles of large calibre and simple build intended for use by the frontiersmen. The stocks were normally of walnut and of half-length, with iron or (more rarely) brass furniture; although a patchbox was rarely included amongst the furniture, double set-triggers were often fitted. The heavy octagonal barrels varied in length from 28–38in and bore diameter ranged from 0.40in to 0.68in; the average 30–32in barrel of 0.52in calibre carried a $\frac{1}{2}$oz ball, with a charge of 100–120 grains of powder ($3\frac{3}{4}$–$4\frac{1}{2}$ drams). These, the most powerful muzzle-loading rifles made in America, were used against the continent's most dangerous game and for defence against Red Indians. Although the Sharps and a few of the other capping breech-loaders made some inroads on the popularity of these rifles, they were not wholly replaced until the large-calibre Sharps cartridge rifles appeared in the first half of the 1870s. In the European sense these rifles were not strictly sporting rifles, as they were tools in the same sense as the spade or the knife and intended as a fundamental aid to survival amongst a hostile wilderness.

The copper cap was the only form of percussion ignition to achieve widespread popularity in America, although the pill-lock and tape-lock both saw limited use. There were, however, several mechanisms utilising the copper cap which saw far more use in America than elsewhere; the most important of these were the side-striking hammer or 'mule-ear' lock and the underhammer system in which the trigger-guard bow acted as the mainspring—a type particularly popular in the New England states on both sporting and target rifles.

The American sporting rifles' rifling, whatever their external style, tended to be of a single basic form with a wide variation in the twist and depth according to the type of projectile to be used and the whim of the maker. This was the old angular Germanic rifling in which the square groove was about half the width of the land, and up to 0.015in in depth. The number of grooves varied, although generally an odd number rather than an even one, and seven was the most common. The twist or spiral of the rifling averaged about one turn in 48in, but larger calibres tended towards slower pitches—for example 1 turn in 120in—so that high velocity with heavy powder charges could be developed without the patched ball stripping the rifling. Rifles intended for an elongated projectile of some type (and most New England percussion rifles were made for a 'sugar-loaf' or 'picket' bullet) had a more rapid twist, one turn in 30in or 36in but sometimes as rapid as one turn in 20in or 24ins.

American sporting rifle sights were, almost without exception, of the plain open type with both the foresight and the rearsight dovetailed into the barrel to enable crude windage adjustment to be made by tapping the sight base. A brass or, less commonly, iron blade served as foresight.

In Britain, while manufactured in far smaller numbers, there evolved a fascinating variety of sporting rifles each designed to suit shooting of a particular sort. By the time of the percussion period all tended to follow a basic pattern: a half-length stock, an octagonal barrel with a rib and a ramrod beneath, and a bar-lock with a sliding safety catch locking both the hammer and the tumbler in the half-cock position. The wrist was usually chequered, although the fore-end was sometimes left plain, and the trigger-guard usually incorporated a scroll or spur which acted as a pistolgrip. Eyes for sling swivels were mounted on the upper ramrod pipe and on the underside of the butt. Double-barrelled rifles increased in popularity through the percussion period, and normally followed the style of the contemporary sporting guns, except that a circular capbox was let into the right side of the butt, the scroll or spur guard and sling eyes were fitted, and safety bolts were added to the locks. Later double rifles made from the mid-1850s often have a full pistol grip stock.

Two distinct markets for British sporting rifles emerged during this period that had not been so clearly defined in the age of the flintlock: the home or domestic market, which included deer stalking rifles and 'rook-and-rabbit' rifles, and the colonial market which included rifles for thin-skinned game and big-game rifles—both of which were needed in India and Africa. A third market, the export trade, required the production of cheap rifles for the North American and South African markets well into the 1880s; in both instances the guns tended to follow the basic designs of indigenous weapons.

Rook-and-rabbit rifles were primarily single-barrelled weapons, virtually reduced-scale versions of the larger deer-stalking rifles. They varied in calibre from 0.300in to about 0.400in and used polygroove or two-grooved rifling; they fired small charges of powder and were usually sighted for ranges from 35 to 110yd, with multi-leaf rearsights. Their quality and finish is usually lower than that of the larger rifles and their survival rate is correspondingly lower.

The mainstay of the British home market was the deer-stalking rifle. From the early percussion period into the 1850s these were single-barrelled rifles of from 13 to 18 bore (0.71in to 0.63in calibre) intended for powder charges not exceeding $2\frac{1}{2}$ drams (70 grains) and often less. The average bore size was 16 bore, or 0.66in calibre. Rifling varied according to the preference of the purchaser or the recommendations of the maker, but the most common types were the rounded-groove multi-groove pattern (usually made with eleven grooves) and the two-groove or 'Brunswick' style. The former had from a half to a full turn in the barrel's length, while the two-groove copied the Government system in having a full turn. Barrel lengths varied from 28 to 36in, with an average value of 30in, although fashion seems to have dictated both very long and very short barrels at times.

Within the general overseas market for British sporting rifles of the percussion era, there were subdivisions based largely upon the type of individual for whom the weapon was intended. In the first instance there were the gentlemen sportsmen who sailed for Africa or India equipped with a veritable arsenal of arms for all types of game. These arms tended to be of the finest quality in both decoration and finish, and were constructed along lines established for their particular purpose. In the second instance there was the resident colonial who ordered British weapons made for local use—and these arms tended to be of far lower quality in both finish and decoration, although often more stoutly built and more structurally sound than the more elegant weapons of the visiting sportsman. Weapons purchased by officers on colonial duty, of which there appear to have been a considerable number, fall between the two extremes; a favourite device was to have one stock with interchangeable rifle and sporting gun barrels, and when the Minié system came into use in the early 1850s the barrels were often made in 0.577in calibre to accept the readily-obtainable Government ammunition.

The majority of rifles made for use on thin-skinned game were double-barrelled, with barrel lengths from 26 to 32in and barrels of 32 to 24 bore

(0.52in to 0.58in calibre). The rifling was again either of the two-groove or the multi-groove pattern and, in addition, rifles made after the 1850s occasionally had shallow rectangular grooving in imitation of the Enfield rifling. Some of these latter arms also had the much slower twist of 1 turn in 78in, the Government standard. Some barrels have outright copies of the Government three-groove rifling.

Rifles intended for lion and tiger shooting were also normally double-barrelled but they usually had shorter and heavier barrels of increased calibre. The average barrel length of these guns was 24–28in, with calibres of 16–10 bore (0.66in–0.77in), as often as not of the two-groove pattern. With rifles of this general description there was an increased use of one smoothbored barrel in conjunction with one rifled one, as the former allowed the use of a very large powder charge for the short-range smashing power often required to ground a wounded beast.

Big-game rifles were made in calibres from 10 to 4 bore—occasionally even larger—and in both single and double-barrelled types. These massive rifles tend to have multi-groove rifling and many are of the type correctly known as the 'Elephant Gun', with very heavy smoothbored barrels for firing truly tremendous powder charges and exploding bullets. In design they are virtually enlarged versions of the standard patterns, although generally neither as highly finished nor as beautifully decorated as the smaller game rifles.

Whether single or double-barrelled, British sporting rifles were usually fitted with a series of individually-hinged leaf sights inlaid at the centre-lines with platinum or gold, and which lay flush with the top of the barrel or the rib. Some rifles had a series of leaves, all of which lay flush so that the gun could be fired at point-blank range without elevation or—in the case of combination guns with one smooth and one rifled barrel—so that the smooth barrel could be fired as a sporting gun with small-shot. When graduated, as many sights were not, the ranges rarely exceeded 250yd; the average set of sights included a notched block and two leaves, sighted for 50 to 150yd, or 100 to 200yd.

In any attempt to define a particular rifle, unless of very large or very small bore, it must be noted that no hard and fast definitions can be adopted since some sportsmen had strong individual views while others would be guided by the gun maker's recommendations. A certain amount of guidance is, however, furnished by the decorative motifs found on the rifles: for example stags on deer-stalking rifles, and lions or tigers on rifles intended for this type of animal. Cheaper quality weapons lack this type of identification and were, in the course of events, utilised for a wider variety of shooting than the more costly and specialised guns.

The majority of Continental percussion sporting rifles were very light in weight compared to their bore size, were heavily carved and decorated, and used the old angular deep rifling so typical of Germanic flintlock rifles. There were individual exceptions, of course, which included the heavy double-barrelled German boar rifles, which often had provision for a hunting bayonet, and the single and double-barrelled Austrian chamois rifles. These tended to be plainer and heavier. German and

Austrian rifles usually had full octagonal barrels and double set-triggers. French and Belgian rifles had either octagonal or round barrels and a plain trigger or, sometimes, a single set-trigger. With the exception of mountainous shooting in Alpine areas, most Continental rifle shooting of the percussion period was conducted by driving; the ranges were not great, nor was there the necessity for carefully placing a killing shot when other shooters were at hand to despatch a wounded animal.

20. A Pennsylvania longrifle, c. 1850. Most of the percussion rifles of this style are flintlock conversions; the trend during the percussion period was to half-length stocks and ornate brass furniture. These late rifles have a narrow butt with a deeply-curved buttplate; double set-triggers are standard and the form of the lock and drum nipple seat are typical.

21. An Ohio Valley rifle, characterised by the half-length curly maple stock, ornate brass furniture and German silver fore-end cap and key plates. Sidelocks were used as often as the back-action lock on this example. The barrel is stamped J. C. GRUBB PHILA and the lock bears JAS GOLCHER with scrollwork and partridges. The patent breech with snail is an unusual refinement. *Barrel length 34¼in, calibre 0.30in, rifled with 6 square grooves making ⅔ turn in the barrel length.*

22. A New England rifle, probably of Belgian make, retailed by MOORE & BAKER of New York, and so stamped on the barrel. German silver furniture is used throughout, and the stock is of walnut; amongst the German silver inlays are a running deer on the cheek-

rest, a brace of grouse on the left wrist, a fish formed as an extension to the lockscrew cup, and an eight-pointed star to the rear of the cheek-rest. The openwork patchbox is crudely engraved with a running deer scene and the release for the patchbox is on the tang of the buttplate. The finely chequered wrist, single trigger and scroll guard are also typical features of this type. The barrel has a break-off breech, and the lockplate is stamped R. S. CLARK EXTRA. *Barrel length 37¾in, calibre 0.36in, rifled with 7 square grooves making 1 turn in the length of the barrel — indicating probable use of an elongated bullet rather than round ball.*

23. A very typical example of a full stocked rifle manufactured in England and imported in large numbers by numerous American retailers in the period 1850–80. The stock is of deeply stained ash and the furniture is brass, except for the German silver escutcheons. The sidelock is stamped H. T. COOPER (New York c. 1845). The single trigger is of brass. *Barrel length 32¹⁵⁄₁₆in, calibre 0.42in, rifled with 7 squared grooves making ½ turn in the length of the barrel.*

24

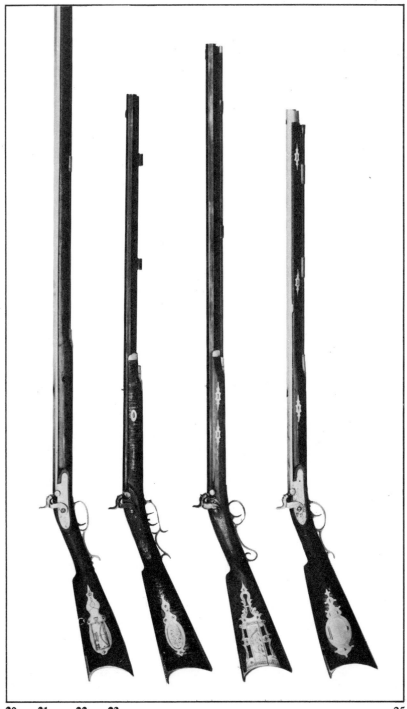

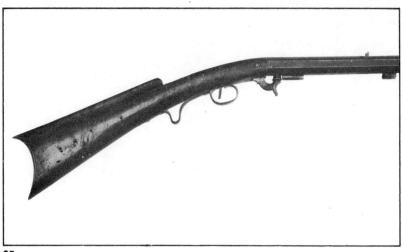

25

24. A Plain rifle by Samuel Hawken of St. Louis. The Plain rifle was a late development of the longrifle, characterised by a short barrel of large calibre and fitted with iron furniture, and of simple stout construction. This early full-stocked example by Samuel Hawken of St. Louis (Missouri) is a conversion from flintlock, later examples normally have a half-stock.

25. A Vermont Underhammer rifle, by Nicanor Kendall of Windsor, Vermont, c. 1840. The barrel is stamped N. KENDALL, WINDSOR, VT. PATENT and numbered 302, while the tang is stamped SMITH'S IMPROVED STUD LOCK. This is a typical New England underhammer design, made without a fore-end, with brass furniture and single trigger. The mechanism is attached to a brass plate on the underside of the butt ahead of the trigger guard. The hammer acts also as a tumbler. *Barrel length 24¹⁵⁄₁₆in, calibre 0.40in, rifled with 7 square grooves making 1 turn in 48in.*

26. The typical 'English' sporting rifle of the period 1830–50 has a full octagonal browned twist barrel of 28–32in, a bar-lock with a sliding safety

26

bolt, a half-length stock with blued iron furniture, and a horn fore-end cap; it is often found with a circular patch or capbox in the butt. The form of the trigger guard—called a spur guard—acts as a pistol grip and replaces the earlier scroll guard. The true pistolgrip became popular at a later date.

27. A double-barrelled deer-stalking rifle by William Moore & Co. of London typifies the British double rifle used in the 1840–70 period for deer-stalking and for thin-skinned game of similar size in India and Africa. This example dates from the mid–1850s and is of 16 bore with two-groove rifling. It is sighted to 300yd.

28. An 8 bore double rifle by W. & J. Rigby. African and Indian game of the dangerous types (such as lion, tiger, and leopard), but lacking the size and endurance of the larger species, were often shot with weapons similar to this double rifle. The eight wide, shallow grooves of the rifling make only one half turn in the barrel length of the 28¼in, indicating the use of a large charge of powder. The rifle is sighted to 200yd.

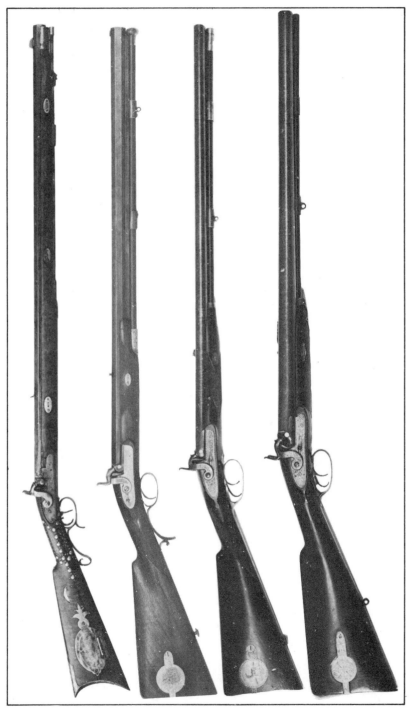

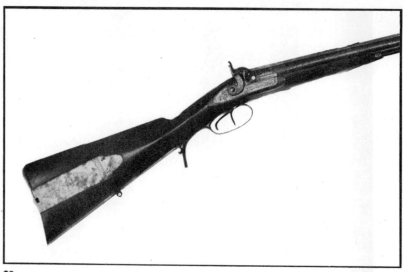

29

29, 30. The 'Cape rifle' often has one barrel smoothbored and the other rifled, but this 0.500in calibre example retailed by John Hayton of Grahamstown has both barrels rifled with two grooves. This was a standard and popular form of rifle in South Africa. The 1in wide rib has a set of lines one inch apart, inlaid with German silver and numbered from 1 to 20, which was used for measuring the spread of trophy horns. The rearsight, which fits over the rib and slides along it, was removed for safe-keeping and kept in the butt-trap; this was also done so that the rifle could be used for point-blank shooting without a sight.

31. A 6 bore rifle by W. G. Rawbone of Cape Town. Rhinoceros, hippopotamus, Cape buffalo and elephants demanded the utmost in knock-down power to avoid either the charging or the escape of wounded animals. Since more metal could be concentrated in the barrel of a single rifle than in a double rifle of comparable size, the really heavy rifles were usually singles. The 32in barrel measures 1⅛in across at the muzzle, and the bore is rifled with ten wide grooves making ¾ turn in the barrel.

32. An 8 bore 'double carbine' by

Frederick Barnes & Co. of London. An alternative to the massive 4 and 6 bore rifles was offered in the form of a somewhat smaller double carbine, smoothbored and heavily loaded, which was fired into the animal from horseback at very close range. The sportsman then retreated as required by circumstances, reloading in the process, and returned to repeat the procedure until the quarry expired. This 8 bore example has 24in barrels and no rearsight; a swivel ramrod and a flat-fronted guard bow materially assisted the mounted sportsman in loading and handling the weapon.

33. English single-barrelled sporting rifles with full pistol grip stocks are uncommon; they are normally fitted with a spur guard. This rifle is by Richard Pritchett, the designer of the Pritchett bullet first adopted by the Government for the P/53 rifle-musket. It is made for the Pritchett bullet with broad, shallow, three-groove rifling. The barrel is round and heavy, with a full length flat on top. The leaf rearsight is optimistically graduated to 1,000yd. Single set trigger. This rifle was made in 1854–5. *Barrel length 28in, calibre 0.577in, rifled with 3 broad shallow grooves making ½ turn in the length of the barrel.*

28

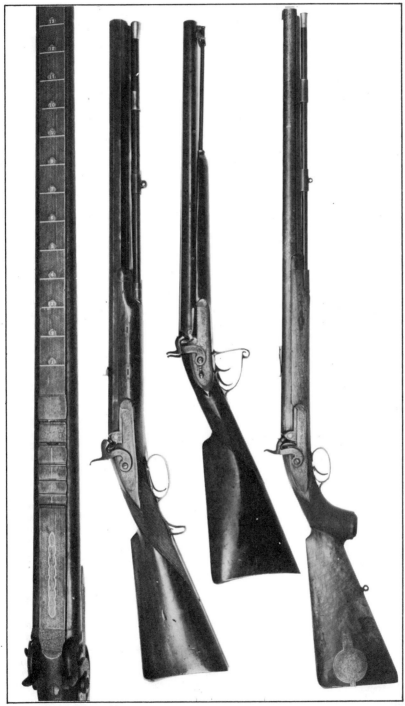

Sporting Rifles

34. A double rifle made by Hollis & Sheath and retailed by James Aston of Hythe, typical of the type made for officers on colonial duty. It is strongly and plainly built without engraving aside from border lines, with a plain walnut stock, and a rearsight strongly resembling the service pattern and graduated to 1,000yd. The breeches are fitted with musket nipples to take the Government cap. The bronze mould casts an Pritchett-Enfield bullet as shown in the compartment at the left side of the case. As Armourer to the School of Musketry James Aston was excellently placed to cater to the needs of officers, and appears to have done so on a large scale. *Barrel length 28in, calibre 0.577in, rifled with 3 broad shallow grooves making ⅓ turn in the length of the barrels.*

35. An Austrian double rifle by the Viennese maker Mathias Nowotny, c. 1845. An elegant and highly decorated rifle featuring stags and chamois; the patchbox cover is of wood veneered with stag-horn, and the scroll guard is made entirely of wood. The style and quality are typical of best Austrian work in the mid–1850s. *Barrel length 26in, calibre 0.61in, rifled with 12 shallow square grooves making ½ turn in the barrels' length.*

36. French double rifle by Le Page of Paris, 1826. The browned barrels are inlaid with gold and are numbered 30

2975. The steel furniture is engraved with foliage, and the steel ramrod is fitted with a brass tip; the 0.61in calibre barrels are hair-rifled and designed to be fired with a relatively small charge of powder and a very tightly fitting patched round ball. The shape of the locks, hammers and breeches is typical of French and Belgian arms of the converted-flintlock and early percussion period, while the absence of the neo-Gothic stock carving is unusual.

37. German double boar rifle by F. Morgenroth of Gernrode-in-Anhalt, c. 1825–30. The 29¼in full-octagonal browned barrels are inlaid in silver on the rib with the maker's name. The gold inlaid locks have the tails formed as boar's heads and the hammers carved as dragons. A common feature of German sporting and military arms of the early percussion period is the combined cap holder and safety, held in position by a spring on the lock. Another feature typical of many percussion double rifles—particularly of German or American origin—is that the barrels are differently rifled: the right barrel of 0.60in calibre has 8 grooves, while the left barrel of 0.61in has 16 grooves. In addition, some are found with the second barrel straight-rifled. The trigger guard and buttplate of this rifle are of horn and only the right lock is fitted with a single-set trigger.

Sporting Rifles

38. A Bavarian wender rifle, of the pattern popular with chamois shooters, by F. Baader of Munich, c. 1850. By pressing back on the catch in front of the trigger guard, the barrels are released to pivot. One barrel—26in in length—is of 0.52in calibre rifled with 7 grooves and the other is 0.56in, smoothbored for use with a ball and large charge of powder or shot. This type of rifle was also popular in America, where they were known as swivel-breech or 'roll-over' rifles and normally made with one rifled and one smooth barrel. The ramrod is carried on the left side between the barrels. The furniture is of iron and fully engraved with foliage and the locks and barrels are gold inlaid. The grip behind the trigger guard is of carved wood.

39. A Belgian rifle by G. Schanne of Herve, c. 1825. This style retains many features of the flintlock, and—indeed —Schanne is known to have worked as early as 1800. The stock is of typical form, with the end of the grip carved as a deer's head. The guard bow and buttplate tang are engraved with dogs, apparently greyhounds. The fine twist barrel is of very light weight. The rearsight has a vertically sliding notch piece secured by two screws. The foresight is a silver blade. The construction of the breech suggests that this rifle was fabricated from unfinished flintlock parts, although the lockplate is not a conversion. *Barrel length 32¾in, calibre 0.52in, rifled with 7 rounded grooves making ½ turn.*

40. A very lightweight Belgian rifle, possibly intended for ladies' use. Although of later origin, the rearsight of this rifle is of the same exact type as the one in Plate 39 and has many of the same structural characteristics, although of inferior execution. The carving of the deer's head is virtually identical, but the engraving of the iron mounts is very crude, and the quality of the barrel is inferior to the Schanne rifle. The back-action lock was much used on Belgian percussion arms. *Barrel length 26¾in, calibre 0.61in, rifled with 12 shallow rounded grooves making ½ turn in the length of the barrel.*

41. A German boar rifle made in the 'English' style, and with a cross-eyed stock, made for the Marquis of Clanricard by Weber & Schultheis of Frankfurt-am-Main, c. 1860. The butt is offset so that a right-handed man could fire with his left eye aligned with the sights. The two-leaf backsight, graduated for 80 and 130yd, is dovetailed into the rib. The ramrod has a deeply cupped tip indicating that a bullet rather than a ball was used. The iron furniture is engraved with boar, dogs and deer, and the capbox has a tiger being attacked by dogs. This is a piece of particular interest, not only for the amount of skilled fitting required but as an indication of the degree to which gun makers could copy the styles of other countries. *Barrel length 27¾in, calibre 0.62in, rifled with 4 grooves making ½ turn in the length of the barrel.*

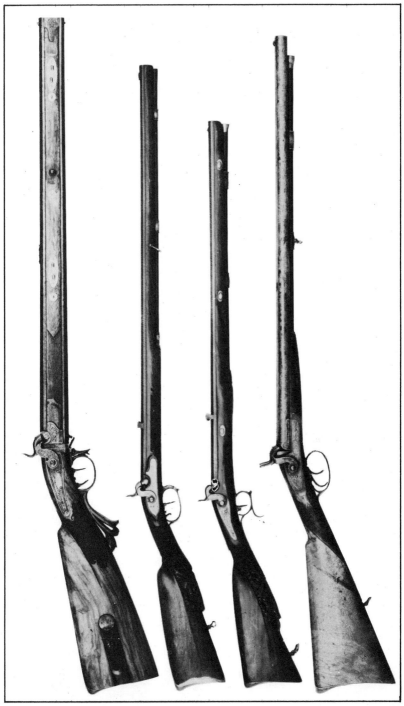

Target Rifles

The most proficient and scientific target shooting of the early percussion era took place in Switzerland, in the South German states, and in the western provinces of Austria. Here the development of rifling systems, projectiles, sights, lock and trigger mechanisms produced the highest degree of accuracy. The rifles, known as schützen or scheutzen rifles, were fired from the standing ('offhand') position at ranges normally about 200yd, and rarely beyond three hundred. To a lesser degree shooting was done from a rest and here again special forms of rifles with extremely heavy barrels were utilised. French target shooting, although developed on a far smaller scale, followed similar lines; the rifles were often imported or constructed locally along the same general pattern, although lacking the extreme specialisation in stock design typical of the Germanic rifles, which had heavy deeply-curved iron buttplates and massive cheekrests.

In the course of the percussion period, American target shooting followed two concurrent paths in different parts of the country. In the north-east target rifles evolved as a separate type of specialised gun entirely distinct from the hunting rifle then in use. While the latter were small calibre half-stocked weapons with plain open sights, generally designed either for the spherical patched ball or for the 'sugar-loaf' or 'picket bullet', the target rifle was built on a much larger plan. Although early examples were fully stocked these soon gave way to rifles without a fore-stock, in which a wooden butt was fitted to a massive octagonal barrel of large calibre. These huge rifles—often weighing more than twenty pounds—normally fired one of several forms of elongated bullet, which were sometimes made in two or three pieces and swaged together: this made it possible to vary the composition of the metal used for the several parts of the bullet. The sights were elaborate, although less mechanically intricate than those on the Germanic rifles, and often took the form of a full length tube sight (or, more rarely, a telescope sight), with both windage and elevation adjustment. A few examples of this type were made with their own shooting bench into which the rifle fitted, to be adjusted with a variety of screw devices. A bewildering selection of tools and accessories accompanied one of these ballistic instruments and some extremely fine shooting was done with them, usually at ranges up to 220yd.

In Pennsylvania and the southern states the target rifle more closely followed the design of the 'Kentucky' or Pennsylvania longrifle except that it was larger, heavier, and had improved sights. Tube sights were unusual and telescopes rarely used, although a normal refinement was the fitting of a pair of elongated hoods which fitted over the barrel to cover the foresight and the rearsight. Some rifles were fitted with a rudimentary aperture sight screwed into the top of the wrist just behind the barrel tang. The full-length stock was sometimes formed with a flat section which, near the muzzle, mated with the flat surface which served as a rest, and a few of these rifles were actually made with the 'foot' or rest fitted as an integral part of the stock. In Beef Matches and Turkey Shoots this type of rifle was capable of excellent shooting at distances of 50–150yd, although the results with the spherical patched ball common to these guns were not generally comparable to the accuracy obtained with the elongated and hardened projectiles of the New England target rifles.

It is interesting to note that this same style of heavy large-calibre rifle fitted with a full stock, with hooded and aperture sights and often with double set-triggers, was also used in Scandinavian target shooting during this period.

The transition in Britain from flintlock to the percussion system, for the target rifle at least, almost exclusively concerned the copper cap. Those who devoted their leisure hours to firing at targets were interested more in ballistic performance—and therefore in the barrels—than in the locks of their guns. Some had tried the Forsyth lock when it first appeared, but most apparently retained the flintlock until the copper cap had been perfected in the late 1820s. There was doubt in many minds whether the more rapid ignition of the percussion system, when applied to rifles, was a good idea. Until the late 1850s the sport of target shooting was conducted by a very small number of moneyed amateurs, who, organised into small local clubs, regularly met to compete for prizes at ranges from 100 to 350yd. Their rifles closely followed the style of the current sporting rifle: a half-stocked gun with an octagonal barrel, of large bore with a rapid pitch of rifling, and firing a tightly-fitting patched ball. There was some experimentation with a variety of oddly-shaped projectiles, but none except the 'sugar loaf' bullet achieved much popularity. Target rifles were normally fitted with a single set-trigger, and had slightly improved sights—usually in the form of a shade over the foresight and in the addition of an aperture tang sight, with or without windage adjustment in addition to elevation. When, in 1837, the British Government adopted the two-groove or Brunswick rifling, this form became popular with target shooters and some excellent shooting was achieved with rifles built on this system. Simplicity of line, elegance of engraving and finish characterised the British target rifle of the percussion period, features common also to the sporting rifle.

The ballistic revolution caused by the general adoption of the Minié system in the early 1850s had tremendous repercussions in the target shooting world. Political and diplomatic events created widespread interest in military marksmanship, now that the rifle had been issued to the entire infantry. An invasion scare, postponed only by cooperation with France in the Crimean War, obliged the Government to allow the formation of Volunteer forces. Target shooting now became primarily a matter of military efficiency and at the same time expanded into a national passtime Target rifles became close copies of the current military weapons, especially of the P/53 Rifle-musket and the P/56 Short Rifle, and particularly of the latter, the arm of the élite Rifle Brigade. Shooting was now commenced at 200yd and extended to 600yd. At the end of 1859 the National' Rifle Association was founded to organise and encourage the development of volunteer rifle shooting and grounds were obtained at Wimbledon with ranges to 1,000yd. Inconsistent shooting of the Enfield rifle—as early as 1854—had brought into the field of experimental ballistics Joseph Whitworth, an eminent engineer, and in 1859 his firm commercially marketed the first of a series of small-bore (0.451in calibre) military and target rifles which were to set the world's long-range accuracy standards for a decade, and which established the fundamental pattern of ballistic development for the many variations of Whitworth's ideas produced by most of the leading contemporary gun makers. Precision marksmanship, although temporarily eclipsed, continued to develop concurrently with military marksmanship and, when the Volunteer ardour had cooled somewhat, there was sufficient interest in the latter field for a schism to occur. In 1864 definitive rules were laid down for the pursuit of the two types of shooting within the control of the National Rifle Association. In the precision shooting field the muzzle-loading percussion match rifle, first introduced by the Whitworth firm late in 1862, retained its grip in Britain until the consecutive defeats of the muzzle-loader by American Sharps and Remington breech-loading rifles in 1874–7 forced the shooters and the gun trade to accept breech-loaders. Military target shooting rapidly turned to the breech-loader from 1865 and from that date the primary interest in target shooting in British circles has always focused upon the military value of such shooting.

Although required by regulations to accept Government 0.577in calibre ammunition, the standard military percussion cap and the regulation sword or socket bayonet, the Volunteer rifle itself presents a large scale study. It represents, with the small-bore match rifle, the two final development stages of the British percussion target rifle. Stock patterns closely copied the P/56 Short Rifle, or the earlier Brunswick or P/51 style with a key-fastened barrel, and were frequently chequered. The mounts also followed the Government pattern, either in iron or in brass, and were occasionally embellished with some degree of mediocre-quality engraving. Somewhat more variety was displayed in the locks, which included plain Government P/53 locks and sporting rifle locks. The sights copied the P/56 elevating type, sometimes with the addition of inlaid centre lines. Apart from the two standard rifling systems adopted by the Government—the 3-groove progressive-depth rifling making 1 turn in 78in and the 5-groove progressive-depth making 1 turn in 48in—Volunteer rifles were also made with Lancaster's gain-twist oval bore rifling, which had been adopted for the Royal Sappers and Miners Carbine in 1855, and a variety of other commercial systems. These included the famous Jacob system with 4 deep grooves, and Major Nuthall's segmental system without angles which was produced by the large-scale makers Turner of Birmingham and Reilly of London, and offered in four, five and six-groove variants.

The small-bore rifle was produced in four basic styles thus: 1, the fully-stocked military rifle with a band-fastened barrel, an iron ramrod and sights (in the military manner) adjustable only for elevation; 2, the essentially similar military target rifle with windage-adjustable sights and mechanically-adjustable elevation; 3, the sporting and target rifle fitted with a half-length stock and most usually found with a pistol grip, an octagonal (or occasionally round) barrel with a rib and a wooden ramrod beneath, a lightweight lock and lightweight furniture as found on the contemporary sporting rifle, and fully-adjustable mechanical sights; 4, the match rifle—the ultimate refinement of the British percussion target rifle—with a half-length pistol grip stock, no ramrod, and a complete set of finely-adjustable target sights normally supplied as a separate cased outfit together with the loading and cleaning equipment. All four styles were rifled upon basically the same principles of an 0.451in bore with the rifling making 1 turn in about 20in, and firing a bullet of about 530 grains with approximately 85–100 grains of powder. The number and shape of the rifling grooves constituted the significant difference between the numerous systems in use.

Target Rifles

42. A Swiss schützen target rifle, converted from flintlock. Originally manufactured in the canton of Thurgau, c. 1815–25, the percussion conversion was instigated in the period c. 1830. Later examples usually have a half-length stock, but all the other features typical of the type are present in this weapon, including the ornate sights and the design of the butt.

43. An American 'New England slug rifle' by Edwin Wesson. Although this example was used during the Civil War of 1861–5 by a Union sharpshooter, the features are typical of such rifles made in the period 1840–90 for long-range bench-rest target shooting. The massive barrel, of 0.45in calibre, is 29½in long.

44. An English target rifle by William Moore of London, 1841. The features which distinguish this class from a sporting rifle include the aperture tang sight which is adjustable for both windage and elevation by the use of a watch key, the provision for a sight shade to slide over the foresight, a single set or hair trigger, and the extra length of barrel. The absence of a cap-box in the butt is typical of target rifles, although some sporting rifles also lack this fitting. *Barrel length 36in, calibre 17 bore, rifled with two grooves making 1 turn in the length of the barrel.*

45. A Brunswick-Enfield Volunteer Rifle by W. & C. Scott, 1859. A good example of the latitude allowed to Volunteers in arming themselves. The rifling is that of Charles Lancaster's oval bore, the calibre and sights—as well as the lock— are of contemporary Enfield pattern, and the stock and furniture follow the lines of the older Brunswick rifle. The rearsight is graduated to 1100yd. *Barrel length 33in, calibre 0.577in.*

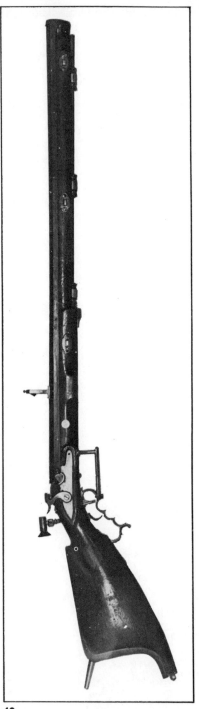

42

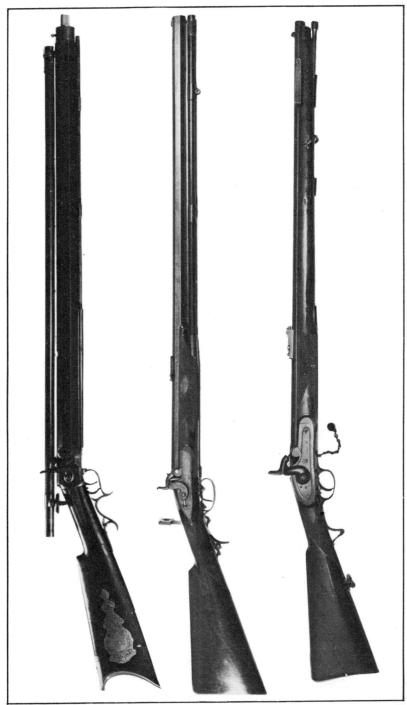

Target Rifles

46. A P/56 Volunteer Short Rifle by William Greener, 1860. A typical example of a Government pattern rifle with decorative modifications. With the exception of the markings and the hammer the arm conforms to the regulation P/56 Short Rifle. The nocksform is engraved with the arms of Tynemouth and the lock bears a Crown over TVRC (Tynemouth Volunteer Rifle Corps). Both the hammer and the style of marking are typical of Greener's Volunteer rifles. *Barrel length 33in, calibre 0.577in, rifled with 3 grooves making 1 turn in 78in.*

47. A P/53 Enfield Volunteer Rifle by Parker, Field & Son, 1862: a prize rifle won for target-shooting proficiency by a member of the 40th Middlesex Volunteers. All of the iron furniture is scroll-engraved and the selected walnut stock is oil varnished and chequered. Although chequering was not uncommon, the long Enfield was rarely given such lavish decoration. No improvements in the sights or the rifling were made on this rifle. *Barrel length 39in, calibre 0.577in, rifled with 3 grooves making 1 turn in 78in.*

48. A small-bore military rifle by Thomas Turner, 1861. With the ex-
40

ception of the bore (Turner's patented rifling) and the structural refinement of the rearsight (which is more finely calibrated but still elevated only by friction), there are no improvements over the service rifle which it superficially resembles. This is the plainest of the several patterns of military target shooting rifles which became popular in Britain from 1860. *Barrel length 36in, calibre 0.451in, rifled with 5 grooves on Turner's principle of decreasing depth and width from breech to muzzle, with a spiral of 1 turn in 20in.*

49. A small-bore military target rifle by Walker of Balgonie. A singular combination of military and match rifle features, with a full-length fore-end secured by Enfield-type clamping bands and fitted with a service pattern ramrod, but with a full pistol grip, sporting lock and capbox—and fitted with target sights (tang sight missing) even to the heel sight fitting for shooting in the back position. The barrel sights are of Alexander Henry's design (foresight removed), and the rearsight is adjustable for elevation by a screw which moves the slide. *Barrel length 33in, calibre 0.451in, rifled with Henry's 1860 patent 7-groove rifling making 1 turn in 22in.*

46,   47,   48,   49

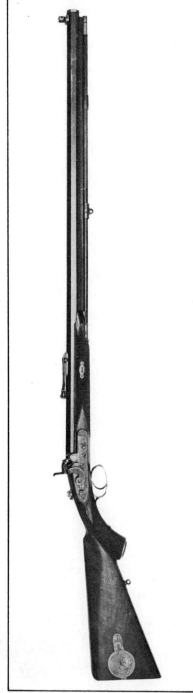

Target Rifles

50. A small-bore sporting/target rifle by Alexander Henry. Henry and Thomas Turner specialised in combining the half-length stock and full octagonal barrel of the sporting rifle with the small-bore patent rifling and refined target sights to produce this popular pattern of target rifle. The idea was to concentrate the maximum permissible weight in the barrel to gain stability, within the 10lb limit set by the National Rifle Association. *Barrel length 34in, calibre 0.451in, rifled with Henry's 1860-patent 7-groove rifling, making 1 turn in 22in.*

51. The Whitworth military target rifle, cased complete, 1860. This, the first Whitworth target rifle, closely followed the lines of the current military rifle, although fitted with refined sights, a lighter lock and decorative embellishments. The plain-blade foresight is dovetailed into the base and, although the rearsight is finely made and calibrated, the slide operates only by friction. Whitworth's patent 'trap-door' cartridge is shown in the centre compartment above the rifle. *Barrel length 33in, calibre 0.451 in, rifled with six grooves in the form of a hexagon, of uniform depth and making 1 turn in 20in.*

52. The Whitworth Match Rifle, 1862. The ultimate development in the design of the English percussion target rifle: it has a half-length stock with a full pistol grip and no provision for ramrod which was carried separately. The foresight is adjustable for windage, and is provided with interchangeable sight elements (furnished in a separate leather case); an aperture tang sight with elevation adjustment on the vernier scale, again with various eye pieces, was also supplied. This has Whitworth's rack-and-pinion rearsight on the barrel. Hardened hexagonal bullets were sold with these rifles. *Barrel length 36in, calibre 0.451in, rifled with six grooves in the form of a hexagon, of uniform depth and making 1 turn in 20in.*

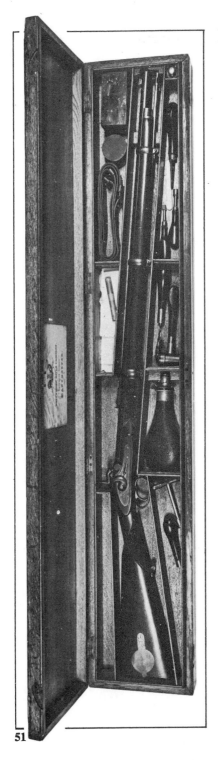

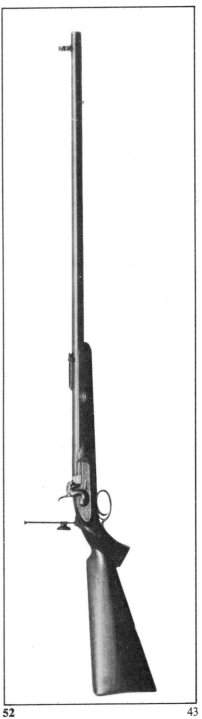

51

52

43

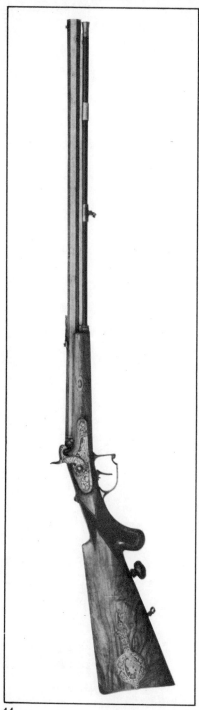

53. A Bohemian sporting/target rifle by Schenk of Marienbad, c. 1860. Basically the design is that of a fine quality sporting rifle, but the top of the wrist is fitted with a tang sight base, there is a single set-trigger, and the knob which is screwed into the underside of the butt behind the pistol grip removes to screw into the end of the ramrod for steady loading of a tightly-patched ball. The rearsight has a screw-adjustable elevation mechanism. The front of the trigger guard bow is made flat to act as a grip for the hand in firing from the hip-rest position favoured by German target shooters. The muzzle and breech of the twist barrel, the lock and the hammer, and the capbox are inlaid with gold in addition to being deeply chiselled and chased. *Barrel length 28½in, calibre 0.58in, rifled with 8 rounded grooves making ¾ turn in the length of the barrel.*

Military Muskets

The adoption of percussion ignition as the standard system for military firearms came considerably later than its general acceptance for sporting and target purposes. It is also important to remember that although a specific date may be given for the official approval or adoption of the system by the authorities of a certain country, the flintlock often remained in the hands of the troops for many years thereafter. The usual practice was for picked regiments—such as the Guards—to be quickly furnished with new weapons, and for other units to receive them as their old arms wore out or when they were called upon to perform specific duties in which the possession of the new arms might prove advantageous.

In addition to the professional standing and prestige of a regiment which determined when it received percussion arms, the structure of the countries' armed forces had also to be considered. There were usually Guards, front line regiments, reserves, militia, frontier guards, police, customs and excise units, various naval categories, mounted branches of the service and the artillery. The older arms—in this instance the flintlock—remained in service for many years in the reserve and militia regiments, and were only ultimately replaced in the event of war or by the eventual trickling down the line of the newer arms—often themselves then obsolescent.

In attempting to establish the actual possession of a specific type of arm by a military unit at a given date, it is extremely important to keep these factors in mind as well as the official dates of adoption and issue.

The excellence of the percussion ignition system as a replacement for the flintlock, was not nearly so evident for military purposes as in the case of civilian arms. In the first place, the various early forms of percussion ignition were somewhat unstable both in their composition and in their durability. Most were delicate or awkward to use, and the mechanisms associated with them were in many instances more delicate than the flintlock. Although the copper cap ultimately proved the most suitable, many had regarded it with doubt during the years in which development took place; the tube-lock was a successful competitor in several countries, amongst them Britain, and Austria actually issued the tube-ignition system between 1838 and 1854. The mass production of the copper cap posed numerous problems, and difficulty was also experienced in waterproofing them for long-storage purposes; the instability of the fulminate also caused considerable difficulty.

A second major consideration was one of finance. Most governments in the early 1830s had stores of flintlock weapons on hand, and it was eminently desirable to devise a system which could be easily adapted to

45

existing arms and to the parts held in store. Where hundreds of thousand of arms were concerned this was no small matter, and it took some time to settle upon a system which was in itself suitable for military issue and which could by virtue of its design be fitted to the extant flintlock weapons.

The sportsman or target shot could afford to tinker with a delicate mechanism; he could be fascinated with the intricacies of a new system; he could spend hours taking it apart and carefully cleaning it after each use to prevent the corrosive fulminate from damaging the small working parts, and he could exercise care in the use of the mechanism when in the field. If something got out of order so it would be returned for repair to the gun maker with perhaps a few caustic remarks, and another gun would come from the rack.

None of these conditions applied to the soldier on active service and, in considering which of the numerous percussion systems was suitable for their services, the governments of Europe had to consider the various combinations of robustness, compactness, simplicity, and durability inherent in each new design. The locks also had to be easy and cheap to repair, and the applications of fulminating compound to certain types of service had to be considered.

Timing presented yet another complication, for when the percussion system came seriously to the notice of the military authorities so, too, did the merits of the rifled bore. Experiments with various projectiles and rifling systems initiated in Switzerland and France in the late 1820s caused a stir in military circles, after the manner of a stone cast into a pond which sends out radiating ripples. If only it were practicable, the general adoption of a rifle by the armed forces would give the nation a tremendous advantage in the exercise of its foreign policy and in the campaigns of the next war; extensive changes would need to be made in the design and use of artillery, and in both strategy and tactics. Could a new ignition system and a long-range projectile used in a rifled bore then be combined when the change from flintlock was ultimately made? In some countries it remained a matter of priorities and as matters developed the percussion system came first, followed by the wider use of the rifle for military purposes.

The flintlock ignition system had been the standard for many years with little cause to question its utility. All military thinking was based upon acceptance of its several liabilities and the smoothbored barrel was considered standard. When the various improvements—each with inherent drawbacks—were presented to groups of military men, politicians concerned with the economic realities of the times, and ministers with specific knowledge in neither field (in some instances), it is very easy to understand why the military adoption of the percussion system took as long as it did. In reality, the speed and efficiency with which the changes were carried into effect were admirable.

Although little-known, it is hardly surprising that in 1826 the cantons of Switzerland were the first to adopt the percussion system as standard. It must be noted, however, that their existing store of flintlock arms had not been completely converted to percussion by the early 1850s. The Hanoverian experiments, which commenced in 1828, attracted the most attention in western Europe—although in the summer of 1820 the British Government had conducted trials with Manton's tube-lock and Egg's cap. The table below shows the initial and final adoption dates of the percussion system by the military authorities of the most significant nations of the mid-nineteenth century. The initial dates, at which time new arms were issued in limited numbers for extensive field trials, are shown in brackets, followed by the date at which overall use of the percussion system was officially accepted.

Austria	(1835)	1838	Piedmont	(1833)	1844
Bavaria		1842	Russia	(1839)	1843
Belgium	(1838)	1841	Saxony	(1833)	1835
Britain	(1831)	1836	Spain	(1831)	1839
Denmark	(1830)	1841	Sweden	(1833)	1840
France	(1837)	1840	United States	(1833)	1841
Prussia	(1831)	1839			

With the exception of Austria all of the leading powers adopted a copper cap, but within this general description there was a great variety of individual types. Structural variations fortunately serve to identify many of the otherwise unmarked examples, the chief confusion occurring amongst the lesser German states—most of whom copied French or Prussian designs. Many countries purchased arms of their own design from manufacturers in Belgium even though arms of the same pattern were made at national armouries. This is particularly true of Piedmont, Naples, Russia, and Britain between 1854 and 1862.

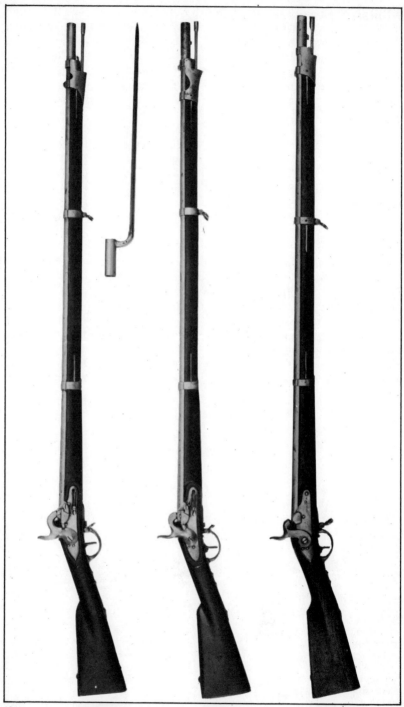

Military Muskets

54, 55. Austrian Models 1838 and 1842 tube-lock muskets. The M.1838 is a conversion of the flintlock M.1828 and retains the original lockplate altered to the Console system; the lockplate is 6½in long. The M.1842 is a new production arm slightly lighter and smaller throughout, although retaining the same basic dimensions. The lockplate (5½in long) is flat with a bevelled edge. Both iron and brass were used for the furniture. After 1844 the date, rendered in the final three digits, appears on the lockplate: earlier arms were usually dated on the barrel. The system is generally known as the Augustin lock, after his improvement of Console's original design. The copper cap was not adopted by Austria until the series of 1854. *Overall length 58in, barrel length 42½in, calibre 0.70 in.*

56. The Bavarian M.1811 musket converted to percussion. This pattern of the conversion continued in use on Bavarian arms—which were manufactured at the State arsenal at Amberg and in Liége—until the slight modifications of the M.1858. Iron furniture. *Overall length 58½in, barrel length 43¼in, calibre 0.70in.*

57. The Belgian M.1841 musket. In 1838 the Belgians began converting their M.1831 flintlock muskets and the variety of other arms in issue to their forces, but the M.1841 was the first new production percussion weapon. The form of the back-action lock and hammer, the reinforce screw through the flat head of the lock, and the break-off breech are typical features of Belgian percussion arms. A small stamp including initials of the setter-up and the final two digits of the date of fabrication appears on the front of the lockplate, and GB in an oval on the barrel denotes Belgian Government ownership. *Overall length 58in, barrel length 42in, calibre 0.69in.*

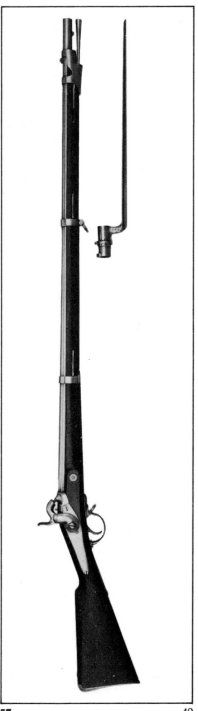

57

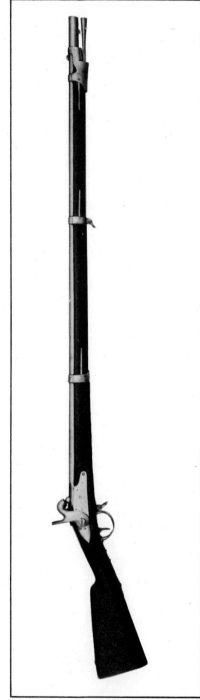

Military Muskets

58. The French M.1822T musket.
Conversion of the M.1822 series began
in 1841, but it was not until 1860 that
the final modification of this model,
rifled on the Minié system, was commenced. The barrel tang is engraved
M^{le} 1822T, while the markings on the
lockplate are those of the original
flintlock. There are several types of
breech design used in converting the
gun, conforming to the then-current
new production arms, the patterns of
1840, 1842 and 1853. All, however, use
the altered flintlock and are designated
M.1822T. *Overall length 58in, barrel
length 42½in, calibre 0.69in.*

59. The French M.1842 musket.
Although the M.1840 was the first new
production percussion arm issued to
the French infantry, it was shortly
superseded by a stronger breech design
in the M.1842, shown here. The style
of the lock and brass furniture was
retained in all subsequent percussion
smoothbore arms, so that a careful
study of the markings and minor
structural changes is required to
distinguish the several subsequent
models. The differences in length of
barrel for various services, established
in the flintlock series, was also retained
(infantry 42¾in, light infantry 40½in,
dragoons 36½in). *Overall length 58in,
barrel length 42⅝in, calibre 0.69in.*

**60, 61. Great Britain's P/39 and P/42
muskets** continued in concurrent production after the appearance of the
latter in 1842; the earlier model was
at first made from old parts originally
intended as flintlocks, and later from
new parts of the old pattern but of
inferior finish compared to those of
the P/42. The P/42 has no sideplate
and has a key-fastened barrel with a
rearsight. While most European
countries adopted the back-action
lock for their percussion arms and
retained band-held barrels, the British
retained both the sidelock and pinned
barrels; the latter was abandoned
only on the P/53 weapons. *Overall
length 55in, barrel length 39in, calibre
0.75in.*

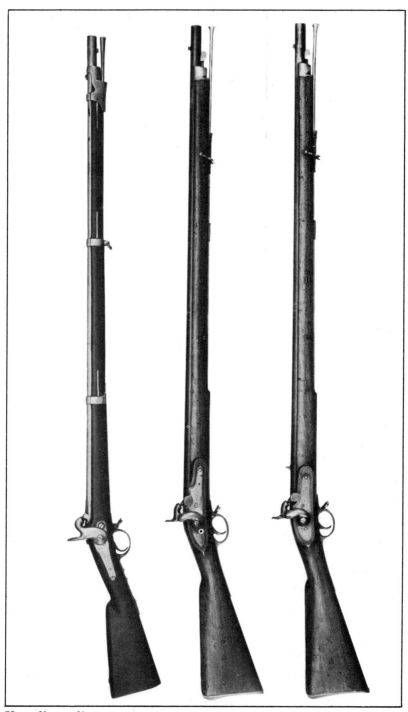

59, 60, 61

Military Muskets

62. The Piedmontese M.1844 musket.
The distinctive feature of Piedmontese percussion military arms is the knob on the hammer spur; they could otherwise be mistaken for French arms. The M.1844 musket was the first new production infantry percussion arm of the Kingdom of Sardinia even though, like the British P/39, it retained an older form of lockplate. Most of these arms were subsequently rifled on the four-groove Minié principle; the result was called the M.1860. They were made in the State arsenal at Torino and in Liége. *Overall length 56in, barrel length 40½in, calibre 0.69in.*

63. The Russian M.1844 musket, a conversion to percussion. The Russians began converting flintlock arms to percussion in 1844, this example being of the M.1839 pattern. A part of the brass pan is left as a support for the nipple lump. The small, narrow butt is typical of both the M.1828 and the M.1839, although it was not continued on the new percussion arms. Each piece of brass furniture is dated and stamped with arsenal mark. *Overall length 57¼in, barrel length 41½in, calibre 0.71in.*

64. The Russian M.1845 musket is an almost-identical copy of the French M.1842, except that the furniture is brass throughout, with each piece stamped with the date and a 'trade-mark' of the particular arsenal. The buttplate tang is engraved with the Imperial eagle and the Imperial cypher. The left side of the butt has a raised cheekrest rather than the French recessed type; the stock is of stained birch, which is typical of all Russian arms. *Overall length 58in, barrel length 42¼in, calibre 0.71in.*

65. The Spanish M.1831 musket, whose production was probably fore-stalled by the Carlist Wars; it was followed by the M.1839, the first production percussion model. This M.1831 has had a new breech fitted and the pan cavity filled with a section designed to act as a water drain. The parts have never been assembled as a flintlock. The barrel bands, sideplate and guard bow are of brass. *Overall length 57⅜in, barrel length 42in, calibre 0.71in.*

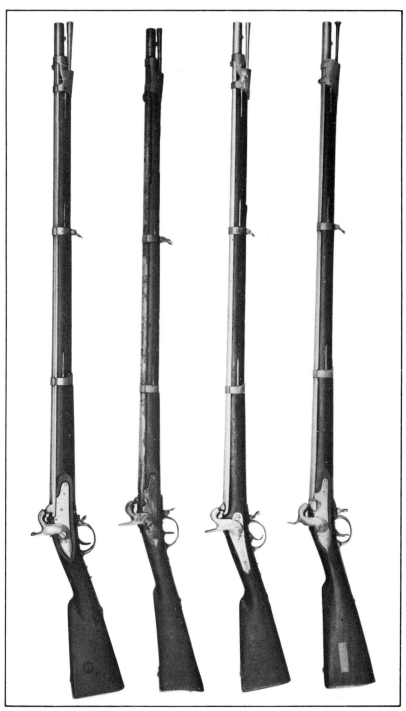

62, 63, 64, 65

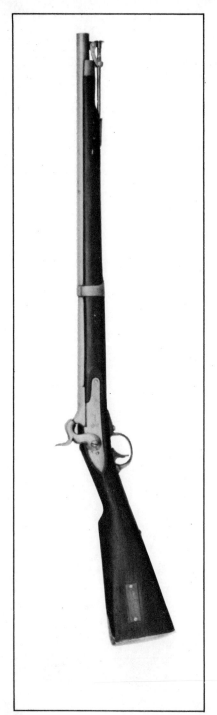

66. A Spanish M.1839 cavalry carbine; an extremely simple design of breech and lock is used, the latter of the same shape as—but not a conversion from —the flintlock M.1836. Flintlock arms of earlier models, notably that of 1828, were still being made in 1841. *Overall length 39in, barrel length 24¾in, calibre 0.71in.*

67. The United States M.1816 musket, converted to percussion after 1848. This is one of three methods of conversion adopted by the American Government. The walnut stock is combless—a feature of this model—and the iron furniture is in the French style. These arms were made at the government arsenals at Springfield and Harper's Ferry, and by numerous private contractors. *Overall length 57⅛in, barrel length 42in, calibre 0.69in.*

68. The United States M.1842 musket: the first new percussion musket issued to American troops, and the last regulation model smoothbore musket. Strong French influence is evident. They were manufactured almost entirely in the two government armouries between 1844 and 1855, and were the first completely interchangeable regulation arms produced by these manufactories with the exception of Hall's breech-loading rifle. Iron furniture was used throughout. The lockplate is stamped with the name of the armoury, U.S., the American eagle and the date of manufacture. *Overall length 57¾in, barrel length 42in, calibre 0.69in.*

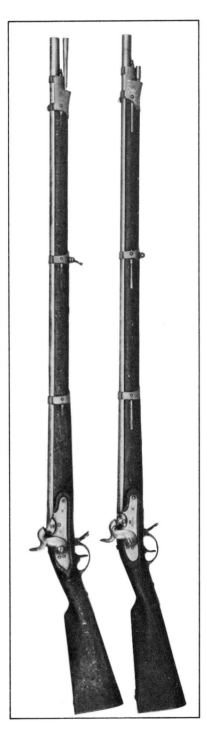

69, 70. The Prussian M.1839 musket.
The fame of the needle-rifle has
obscured the fact that most of the
Prussian army were still equipped
with a muzzle-loading smoothbore
musket, the M.1839 shown here. Plate
69 is the 'Altered M.1839', the flintlock M.1809 fitted with a new breech
and hammer. The lockplate has the
rounded tail terminating in a tit, and
the trigger guard finials and buttplate
tang terminate in points. The new
production Model 1839, Plate 70, has
a new flat lockplate flush with the
wood, and the furniture is rounded
on the surface with plain rounded
terminals to the guard and buttplate.
Both types have brass furniture except
for iron buttplates. In 1855 a large
number of 'New M.1839' muskets
were rifled with five grooves on the
Minié system ; the only external
change was the addition of a hinged-
leaf rearsight graduated to 1,000
paces. This was designated as the
M.1839/55. The stocks are of walnut
or beech. The lockplates bear the
Prussian crown and the name of the
armoury of manufacture, e.g., Potsdam, Neisse, Saarn or Suhl. *Overall
length 57in, barrel length 41½in,
calibre 0.71in.*

Military Rifles

The first recorded use of the rifle in the hands of a small organised group of military marksmen occurred in 1630, when William of Hesse used such troops during the Thirty Years' War. Other German rulers followed suit at various times during the seventeenth century, but all were short-term service units disbanded at the close of a particular war. Frederick II (the Great) of Prussia raised the first permanent corps of riflemen in 1740, and by the beginning of the Seven Years' War in 1756 most European armies included jägerkorps. It is curious to note that the Swedes had armed their ski-troops with rifles as early as 1712. Britain, who had employed several Germanic corps of riflemen during the eighteenth century, did not form her own rifle corps until 1800. In 1804 the very limited use of the rifled bore in the French service was discontinued altogether by Napoleon I, and the rifle was not reintroduced until the percussion era.

Since most of the rifle corps were small and composed of trained marksmen, and since skill in using the rifle to best advantage involved patience and care in loading as well as firing, it was to the rifle corps that most countries issued their experimental percussion weapons.

Until the Swiss and French experiments of the late 1820s, the ballistic development of the military rifle had involved the spherical ball, normally surrounded by a cloth patch. Such a system was ill-suited to rapid loading, and fairly frequent cleaning of the deep grooves was necessary to maintain accuracy. The rifle consequently occupied a limited place in military tactics. When French artillery officers began to experiment with systems involving a smaller-than-bore diameter bullet which, pushed down the bore without a friction-creating patch, was expanded when in the breech to fit the bore and thus gain accuracy, interest was created in military circles.

The systems were basically divided into two types, both of which were adopted by most countries prior to the final step in the development of the muzzle-loading military rifle. Some countries issued both types on rifles of externally identical appearance. The two patterns are the pillar-breech, known also as the 'système à tige' or as the 'Thouvenin system' after the designer, and the chamber-breech or Delvigne system—again named after the French designer. Both types were issued from 1840 and for the next decade one or the other (or sometimes even both) was developed by most European countries. The exceptions were the British, who adopted the plain breech and a deep two-groove rifling with a belted ball, the Russians —who copied the British—and the Swiss, who retained conventional rifling with a smaller bore and a variety of elongated projectiles surrounded with cloth patches.

58

In the pillar-breech rifle a post or pillar was screwed into the face of the breech plug, and the powder was allowed to fill the space around the pillar, extending almost to the top. The bullet slid easily down the bore and stopped when it struck the top of the pillar. It was then dealt one or two smart blows with the heavy iron ramrod which slightly flattened the bullet, thus forcing it into the rifling grooves.

The chamber-breech rifle was made with a long breech plug with a long chamber of smaller diameter than the bore. This was again almost filled with powder, and the bullet came to a halt when it struck the shoulder at the join of the chamber and the bore. It was then struck with the heavy ramrod and expanded into the rifling grooves.

Both systems unfortunately involved distorting the original shape of the bullet, which made accuracy unreliable, and loading time was not much less than the old system of the patched ball. Fouling became less of a problem during loading owing to the reduced diameter of the bullet, but further retarded accuracy as there was no longer a patch to sweep the fouling from the bore.

The 'Brunswick Rifle', adopted by England in 1837 and by Russia in 1843, had no special breech construction and continued to use a composite type of ammunition, with a cloth patch around the ball. The rifling consisted of two deep grooves with the rapid pitch of one full turn in the barrel's length and the spherical ball was made with a belt around its circumference which mated with the two grooves. The theory was that, with the bullet held mechanically by the belt, it could neither strip the rifling from overloading nor from fouling. Two types of ammunition were normally issued with these rifles: the belted ball for accurate slow firing and plain spherical ball for less accurate rapid firing at close quarters. In 1848 the Russians adopted for their rifle a conoidal ball with two studs, probably copied from Charles Lancaster's bullet of 1846.

Important as these developments were in the history of the military rifle, they still failed to make of the rifle a weapon suitable for issue to the line infantry. It was not until the efforts of Delvigne, Tamisier and Minié, all in the French service, produced the cylindro-conoidal expanding-base bullet during the 1840s that the muzzle-loading percussion rifle became a practical weapon for general issue. This system involved a rifling of shallow depth and relatively slow twist, and a bullet having a hollow base, parallel sides and a pointed nose. The diameter of the bullet was smaller than the bore by several thousandths of an inch and was therefore quickly loaded. No action other than seating the bullet was necessary with the ramrod, so that the loading procedure was literally as rapid as the musket. When the powder charge ignited, the expanding gases acted upon the hollow base of the bullet, forced the sides of the bullet into the rifling, eliminated gas escape and forced the ball to take the rifling in its passage out of the barrel —imparting to it the accuracy of the rifle. Since the parallel sides of the bullet could be wrapped in paper soaked in a lubricating mixture, or cut with grooves to contain the mixture, fouling was demonstrably reduced, making frequent cleaning unnecessary and maintaining accuracy for long periods.

The ultimate had been achieved: the accuracy of the rifle combined with the rapidity of the musket. The slaughter inflicted during the Crimean War (1854–6) and, to a greater extent, in the American Civil War of 1861–5 testified to the effectiveness of the new system when employed with older smoothbore tactics. A further improvement was discovered quite by accident: in rifling old smoothbore muskets to the new system it was found necessary to reduce the depth of the grooves as they ran from breech to muzzle, largely because of the thinness of the barrels at the muzzle owing to wear and to the external taper design. It was found that this progressive-depth rifling greatly improved the performance of the Minié bullet and further contributed to the elimination of fouling. The idea was officially adopted by the French on their 1854 series, by the Americans on their 1855 arms and the British on the Enfield series in 1858.

71. The Swiss M.1829 Carabinier's rifle. The Swiss Cantons were the first to adopt the percussion system for their military forces, and this is the first regulation result. Each canton was entitled to issue its own arms provided they conformed to certain standards, including the form of the bayonet bar and the number of grooves to the rifling. The massive furniture is of iron except the finger-grip guard, which is of brass. The wooden ramrod has the Wurstem-berger-system shoulder on the head and a brass tip for seating the bullet. The quadrant rearsight is graduated from 200 to 800 paces. This rifle represents the general pattern of such arms until the adoption of the M.1851 Federal carbine. *Barrel length 35⅜in, calibre 0.62in, rifled with 16 rounded grooves making 1 turn in the barrel.*

72. The Austrian M.1835 Jäger rifle

with first pattern Console lock. The first issue percussion arm of the Austrian service, only the jägers received them in 1835; an improved type was issued in 1838. These are the M.1807 rifle modified to the Console tubelock. *Barrel length 26½in, calibre 0.56in, rifled with 7 rounded grooves making ¼ turn in the length of the barrel.*

73. The Prussian M.1835 Jäger rifle. The first issue percussion arm of the Prussian service, this is an M.1810 rifle converted to percussion. It was known as the 'Potsdam Rifle' and was the first serious attempt to standardise the production of Prussian jäger rifles, the earlier flintlocks having variations in the rifling. The barrel has a slightly chambered patent breech. *Barrel length 28⅜in, calibre 0.60in, rifled with 8 rectangular grooves making ¼ turn in the length of the barrel.*

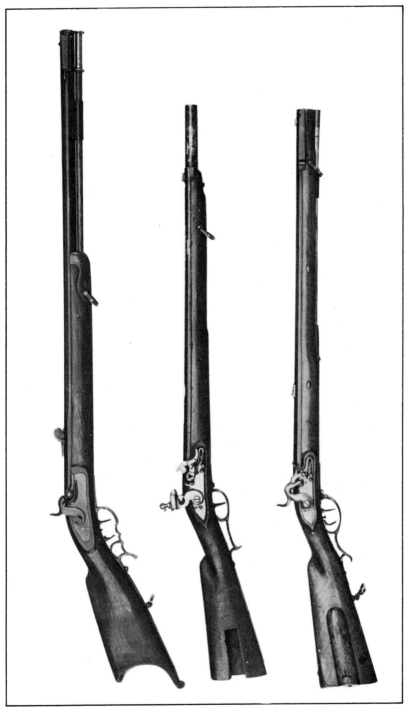

71,   72,   73

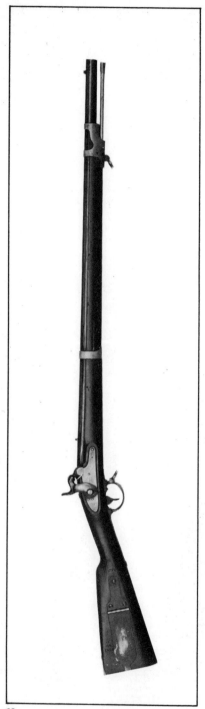

74. The United States M.1841 rifle. The first regulation percussion model adopted by the United States Army, this was followed by the M.1842 smoothbore series. Commonly known as the 'Mississippi' or 'Yager' rifle, it had a long service life. Many were rifled up to 0.58in calibre for use during the American Civil War and fitted with long range rearsights. Not originally fitted with a bayonet, there were several subsequent patterns which required modifications to the barrel and upper band. Brass furniture was used throughout. *Barrel length 33in, calibre 0.54in, rifled with 7 rounded grooves making 1 turn in 72in.*

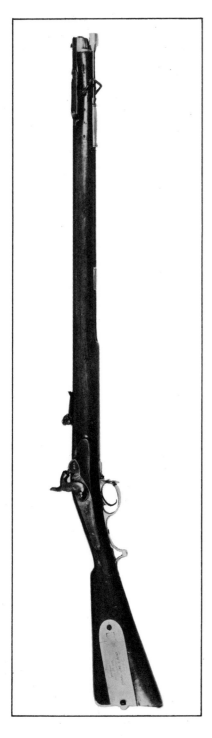

75. The Russian M.1843 carbine for rifle regiments, known as the 'Lüttich Carbine' as it was manufactured in Liége. The first regulation percussion rifle in the Russian service, it was a direct copy of the British Brunswick rifle of 1837. The example shown is of the second type—introduced *c.*1848 —with a quadrant backsight graduated to 1200 paces and a brass-tipped heavily cupped ramrod for use with a winged sugar-loaf bullet copied from Charles Lancaster's bullet of 1846. Many of these rifles were used by Russian sharpshooters during the Crimean War. *Barrel length $30\frac{3}{16}in$, calibre 0.70in, rifled with two deep rectangular grooves making 1 turn in the length of the barrel.*

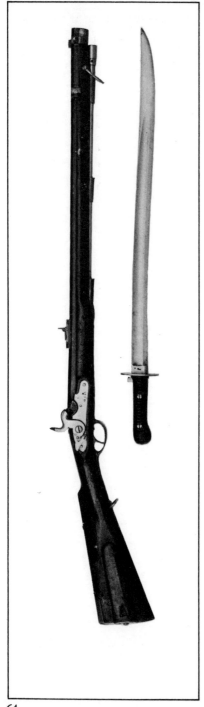

**76. The Dano-Norwegian M.1803/41/
51 pillar-breech rifle.** Denmark and
Norway had vast stores of flintlock
arms in store from the beginning of
the eighteenth century. Rather than
spend money in the design and production of new models, they first converted to percussion the flint weapons
(from 1841), and then in 1851 rifled
certain of them, fitting them with
pillar breeches and a new long range
rearsight. The result is the official
three-date designation. The sight is
graduated from 200 to 600 paces. The
style of conversion is typical for all
types whether rifled or smoothbore,
and the dog-catch was retained by
Denmark, Norway and Sweden
throughout the percussion period on
the majority of their arms. The
furniture is of brass and the birch
stocks are generally painted black.
*Barrel length $28\frac{7}{8}$in, calibre 0.72in,
rifled with 5 wide rounded grooves
making $\frac{1}{2}$ turn in the length of the
barrel.*

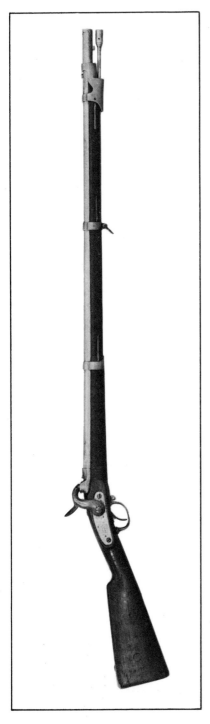

77. The French M.1837 Delvigne-Pontcharra Sharpshooter's carbine. The first experimental issue percussion arm in the French service, it has the chamber breech of Delvigne and used the special sabot cartridge designed by the two men. The furniture is of brass. The shield surrounding the nipple is notched for 150 metres, with a small perforated leaf hinged just ahead of the nipple for longer ranges. *Barrel length 36¼in, calibre 0.72in, rifled with 6 rounded grooves.*

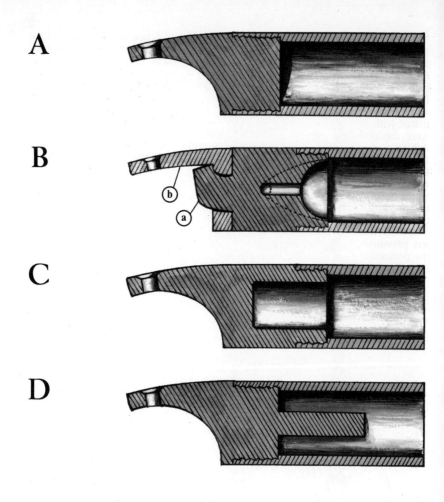

A

B

b

a

C

D

78. Breech types. Figure **A** shows the common or plain breech, with a flat-faced plug and an integral tang screwed into the barrel. **B** shows a patent breech with a break-off or hook; 'patent' refers to the internal form of the plug, two types of which are shown by the dotted lines with the circle at the rear representing the flash channel to the nipple. The break-off is the part marked *a*, which hooks into *b*—the standing or false breech. The hook *a* is sometimes called the 'hut'. **C.** A Delvigne or chamber breech, first introduced in 1840 and widely used on the Continent in the 1840s. There were numerous variations in the shape of the chamber cavity and in the form of the mouth of the breech chamber itself. **D.** The Thouvenin or pillar breech, which first appeared in 1846 on French military rifles and later spread across the Continent until superseded by the Minié system.

79. The development of projectiles, 1830–1860. **A.** Delvigne-Pontcharra, 1831; an early attempt to provide a means of sealing the bore without recourse to a separate patch. **B.** The Brunswick 'belted ball'; the raised section around the centre of the ball mated with the rifling grooves, which were cut deep enough to receive it. Adopted in 1837 by Britain and in 1843 by Russia (see plates 80 and 75). **C.** Delvigne, 1841; an early attempt to provide a means by which the ball could be expanded into the rifling by the pressure of the gas generated by the propellant. **D.** Thouvenin & Minié, 1844; an 'accordion' bullet in which gas pressure compressed the base of the projectile, expanding the lead into the rifling. **E.** Tamisier, 1846; another 'accordion' bullet. **F.** Minié, 1851, the first real step to perfection: the small iron cup in the base of the projectile was forced into the cavity upon firing, consequently forcing the sides of the bullet into the rifling. **G.** Wilkinson-Lorenz; a form of 'accordion' bullet, similar in principle to *D* and *E*, adopted in 1854 by Austria. **H.** Pritchett; an expanding bullet in which the cavity was empty, it was adopted by the British and modified with the addition of a base plug. **I.** Enfield-Pritchett; an improved version of the Pritchett bullet in which a base plug has been added to the cavity to promote more even expansion. **J.** 'American Minié', designed by Burton and officially adopted in 1855. There is no base plug in this design.

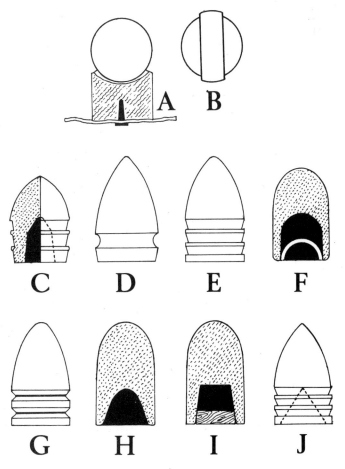

A   B

C   D   E   F

G   H   I   J

Military Rifles

80. The British Brunswick Rifle, first model, 1837. The first percussion rifle of the British Army, it was not actually in the hands of the troops until 1840. The back-action lock was replaced after 1844 with a side-lock. Brass furniture is used. The rearsight is intended for 200 and 300yd. *Barrel length 30in, calibre 0.70in, rifled with 2 deep rectangular grooves making 1 turn in the length of the barrel.*

81. M.1840 'Carabine du Munition' or 'du Thierry'—the first widely used rifle in the French army, provided with a chambered breech on the Delvigne system. The leaf of the rearsight has four apertures intended for use to 550 metres. The iron furniture is of the pattern continued into the breech-loading period. The shape of the breech is typical of all M.1840 weapons. The dividing line of the long breech section may be seen just ahead of the rearsight base. *Overall length 48½in, barrel length 32⅝in, calibre 0.71in, rifled with four rectangular grooves making ½ turn in the length of the barrel.*

82. The Austrian M.1849 chamber-breech Jäger rifle. The single iron barrel band, spring-leaf rearsight graduated to 600 paces, and side-mounted bayonet distinguish this model from the M.1842, which uses the same lock, trigger guard and butt pattern. This example has a Lorenz ramrod. The Austrians retained the Delvigne breech longer than most other countries. *Overall length 48½in, barrel length 33¼in, calibre 0.72in, rifled with 12 round grooves making ½ turn in the barrel.*

83. The French M.1853 Carabine à Tige is identical to the original French pillar-breech rifle M.1846, with the exception of the breech, which on the earlier rifle was that of the M.1842. Note the rearsight, which was widely copied; it is graduated to 1,000 metres. The heavy iron ramrod was used to pound the bullet onto the pillar in the breech, forcing it into the rifling. *Overall length 49⅞in, barrel length 34¼in, calibre 0.71in, rifled with 4 wide rectangular progressive depth grooves, making ½ turn.*

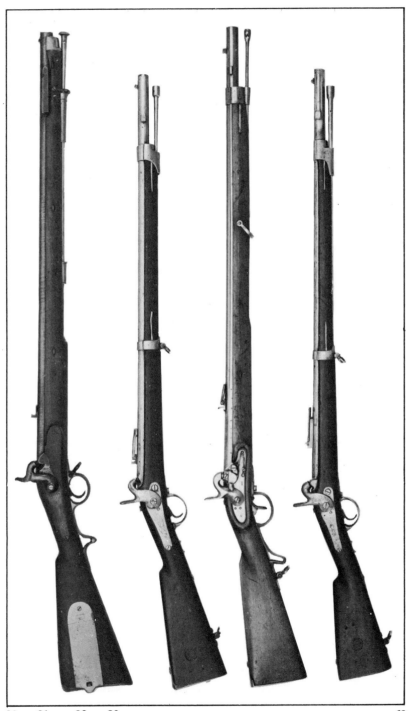

80,   81,   82,   83

Military Rifles

84. The first regulation Minié rifle was the Belgian M.1850, from which the British Government developed its P/51 rifle-musket. Note the key-fastened barrel and the French pattern lock and rearsight; iron furniture was used, including the typically Belgian military feature of a reinforce screw ahead of the lock. *Overall length 55in, barrel length 39in, calibre 0.69in, rifled with 4 rectangular grooves making ½ turn in the barrel.*

85. Britain's P/51 rifle-musket, while retaining the P/42 lock and bayonet locking catch, is a close copy of the Belgian Minié rifle of the previous year. The rearsight is graduated to 900yd and the furniture is of brass. This was the first rifle intended for issue to all line infantry, but the P/53 was put into production before this goal was achieved. The major battles of the Crimean War were over before the majority of the British infantry received rifled arms. *Overall length 55in, barrel length 39in, calibre 0.70*

in, rifled with 4 rectangular grooves making ½ turn in the barrel.

86. The Swiss Federal rifle, M.1851, represented a radical departure in almost all features and was generally acknowledged as the most accurate military arm of its day. But the suitability of such a weapon for any but a small and highly trained army was doubtful: the small bore and rapid pitch of the rifling created considerable fouling problems, and the fragility of the long thin paper cartridge with its elongated bullet wrapped in a tied cloth patch were forceful arguments against its adoption by a larger army. The quadrant rearsight is graduated to 1,000 paces. Iron furniture, double set-triggers, and heavy iron ramrod with a shoulder on the Wurstemberg system were used. These rifles were made in Switzerland and Liége. *Overall length 49½in, barrel length 33in, calibre 0.41in, rifled with 8 rounded grooves making ¾ turn in the barrel.*

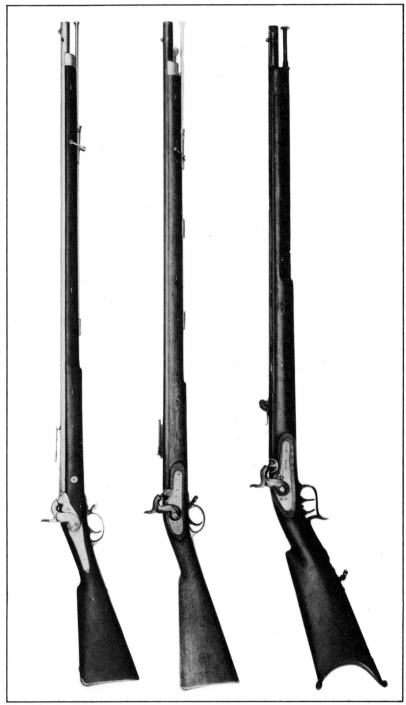

Military Rifles

87. The Bavarian M.1854 Jäger rifle.
One of the last pillar-breech rifles approved before the Minié system swept away all previous types was this Jäger rifle. A curious combination of French and German features, it was fitted with a browned barrel and a rearsight with an automatic windage adjustment on the slide of the leaf, which is graduated to 1,000 paces. This rifle was replaced with the M.1858 rifle of similar design but with a simplified sight and a reduced bore for the Podewils version of the Minié bullet. Iron furniture was used. *Overall length 50½in, barrel length 35¾in, calibre 0.69in, rifled with 4 slightly rounded grooves making ½ turn in the barrel.*

88. The Austrian M.1854 Lorenz rifle for infantry, type II. The Austrians adopted a reduced bore and the copper cap ignition system at the same time, but the bullet was of the 'accordion' design of Wilkinson and Lorenz rather than the hollow base of Minié. The bullet, with deep grooves, had its flat base expanded into the rifling by the explosion pushing the lead forward, rather than sideways as in the Minié system. Type II, in use from 1862 for all infantry rifles, refers to the hinged leaf rearsight ; type I rifles had a plain fixed block sight. Iron furniture was used. The ramrod head has a brass sleeve around it to protect the rifling in loading. *Overall length 52½in, barrel length 37½in, calibre 0.54in, rifled with 4 rectangular grooves making ½ turn in the barrel.*

89. The Russian M.1845 musket, converted 1854. In 1854 Russia began to convert her M.1845 muskets to Minié-rifled weapons. The external changes from the earlier musket include a new ramrod with a heavy deeply-cupped head, and a quadrant rearsight of the pattern used on the M.1843 rifle graduated to 1100 paces. Some 20,000 of these were made up before a new model was adopted in 1856. There were very few rifled muskets in the hands of the Russian forces in the Crimea. *Overall length 58¼in, barrel length 42⅝in, calibre 0.72in, rifled with 4 rectangular grooves making ⅔ turn in the barrel.*

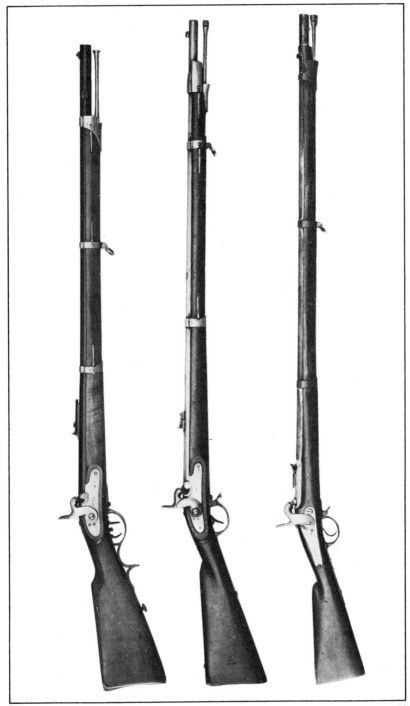

87,   88,   89

90. The Russian M.1856 '6 Line Rifle'
was the first new production rifle
issued to the line infantry and other
branches of the Russian service, and
the first reduced-bore Russian long-
arm. Note the marked change from
French to English influence in the
design, with the Enfield-pattern
clamping bands, swelled ramrod,
hammer and breech form, and the
style of butt. The trigger plate with
the slight curl for better grip is of iron
and the remaining furniture of brass.
The quadrant rearsight is graduated
to 1200 paces. These rifles were made
in Russia and at Liége. *Overall length
53in, barrel length 37in, calibre 0.59in,
rifled with 4 rectangular grooves
making ¾ turn in the barrel.*

91. The United States M.1855 rifle
was the first Minié system arm
adopted in that country, and incorporated the then-popular idea of self-
priming in the form of Maynard's
tape primer—a feature which was
discontinued on the succeeding model.
Until 1858 these rifles were produced
with brass furniture and browned
barrels, and with the large backsight
graduated to 900yd, but in 1858 a
smaller two-leaf sight was adopted
along with steel furniture and bright-
finished barrels. The M.1855 rifle-
musket uses the same lock and furniture, but has three bands and a 40in
barrel. *Overall length 49½in, barrel
length 33in, calibre 0.58in, rifled with
3 rectangular grooves of progressive
depth making 1 turn in 78in.*

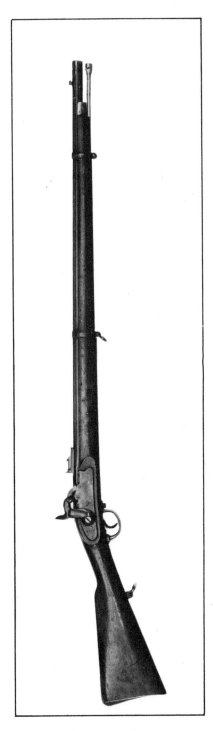

92. The Spanish M.1852 Chasseur's rifle. Spain adopted the Minié system in 1852, and this rifle was the first of the series. The lock has a capguard similar to those used on some earlier German arms and the barrel is browned. The leaf rearsight is similar to that used on Austrian arms and is graduated to 750 paces. Succeeding Spanish models strongly resemble the British P/53 rifle-musket. *Overall length 48¾in, barrel length 33¼in, calibre 0.60in, rifled with 4 rectangular grooves making ⅜ turn in the barrel.*

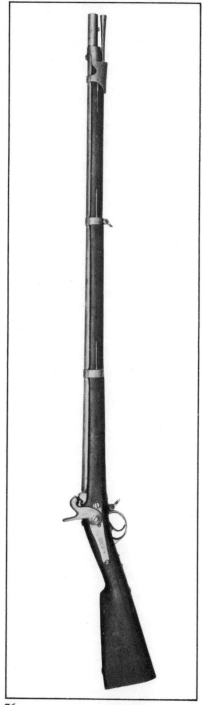

93. The French M.1857 was the first French rifled arm designed to be issued to the entire line infantry, although parts of her forces had been equipped with rifles since 1838. Earlier models — notably the M.1822T, M.1853 and M.1854—were rifled on the same system as the M.1857 from 1858 onwards. The rearsight was the same as that on earlier muskets, as no French musket or rifle-musket was fitted with an elevating rearsight until the breech-loading period. This was the first model in which the longest of the previous series (with a 42½in barrel) was dropped, and the infantry musket thereafter had the 40½in barrel previously used for the light infantry musket. *Overall length 56in, barrel length 40½in, calibre 0.69in, rifled uniformly with 4 grooves making ½ turn in the barrel. The French used progressive depth rifling for rifling smoothbore arms, but found uniform depth rifling more satisfactory on new production.*

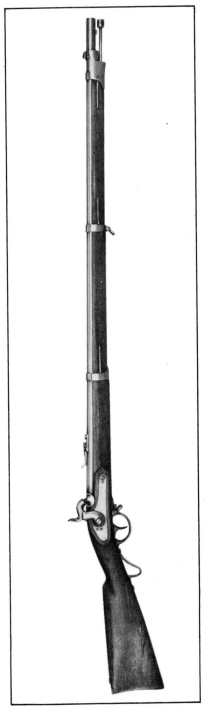

94. The Württemberg Vereinsgewehr of 1856. Between 1856 and 1858 the south German states of Württemberg, Baden and the Grand Duchy of Hesse adopted this *Vereinsgewehr* whose main features were a reduced bore and a Minié-system bullet designed by Bavarian Major Podewils—as well as a complicated tangent sight contributed by Württemberg's Captain Dorn. The furniture was of iron and the lock was of current Swiss pattern. The steel ramrod has a swell, and a brass sleeve over the bearing surface of the head. Most of these rifles were made on contract in Liége, and also in the State manufactory at Oberndorf in Württemberg. *Overall length 55½in, barrel length 39¼in, calibre 0.54in, rifled with 5 rectangular grooves making ¾ turn in the barrel.*

Select Bibliography

Anonymous (United Kingdom Patent Office); **Abridgements of the Specifications Relating to Fire-Arms and Other Weapons, Ammunition and Accoutrements.** *Great Seal Patent Office, London, 1859. Reprinted by Holland Press, London, 1960.*

Bailey, D. W.; 'British Volunteer Rifles 1850–1870', in **Gun Digest.** *Digest Books, Northfield (Illinois), 1972, pages 22–36.*

Bailey, D. W., and Bell, J. B.; 'The Muzzle Loading Small Bore Rifle 1855–1880', in **Guns Review,** *volume 9 number 6, pages 218–224. Ravenhill Publishing Company, Pateley Bridge, June 1969.*

Blackmore, Howard L.; **British Military Firearms, 1650–1850.** *Herbert Jenkins, London, 1961, and Arco Publishing Company, New York, 1962.*

Blackmore, Howard L.; **Guns and Rifles of the World.** *B. T. Batsford, London, 1964, and The Viking Press, New York, 1965.*

Dolleczek, Anton: **Monographie der k.u.k. österr.-ung. blanken und Handfeuer Waffen.** *Originally published in 1896 by Kreisel & Gröger, Wien, and reprinted in 1970 by Akademische Druck- und Verlaganstalt, Graz.*

George, John Nigel; **English Guns and Rifles.** *Small-Arms Technical Publishing Company, Plantersville (South Carolina), 1947.*

Kaufmann, H. J.; **The Pennsylvania-Kentucky Rifle.** *The Stackpole Company, Harrisburg (Pennsylvania), 1960.*

Marquiset, Roger, and Boudriot, Jean: **Armes à Feu Françaises, Modèles Réglementaires 1833-1861.** *Librarie Pierre Petitot, Paris, c. 1965.*

Menges, O. von: **Die Bewaffnung der Preussischen Fusstruppen mit Gewehren (Büchsen) von 1809 bis zur Gegenwart.** *Originally published in 1913 and reprinted in 1969 by J. Olmes, Krefeld.*

Neal, W. Keith, and Back, D. H. L.; **Forsyth & Co.: Patent Gunmakers.** *George Bell & Sons, London, 1969.*

Roads, Christopher H.; **The British Soldier's Firearm, 1850–1864.** *Herbert Jenkins, London, 1964, and Hillary House, New York, 1964.*

Roberts, Ned H.; **The Muzzle Loading Caplock Rifle.** *The Stackpole Company, Harrisburg (Pennsylvania), 1958.*

Schön, Julius; **Rifled Infantry Arms. A Brief Description of the Modern System of Small Arms, as adopted in the Various European Armies.** *Originally Dresden, 1855, this is the English translation of 1860, by J. Gorgas, which appeared in Major Alfred Mordecai's* **Military Commission to Europe in 1855 and 1856,** *Washington, 1860. Gorgas' translation has been separately reprinted: Yorktown (Virginia), 1965.*

Thierbach, Moritz; **Die Geschichtliche Entwicklung der Handfeuer-waffen.** *Carl Hockner, Dresden, 1886–7. Reprinted by Akademische Druck– und Verlaganstalt, Graz, 1965.*